Territorial Ambition

"The Arkansas Traveler," Edward Payson Washburn, Picture Collection, #3934, Special Collections Division, University of Arkansas Libraries, Fayetteville.

Territorial Ambition

Land and Society in Arkansas
1800–1840

S. Charles Bolton

THE UNIVERSITY OF ARKANSAS PRESS

FAYETTEVILLE   2019

ISBN: 978-1-55728-284-2 (cloth)
ISBN: 978-1-68226-128-6 (paper)
eISBN: 978-1-61075-687-7

23 22 21 20 19   5 4 3 2 1

⊛ The paper used in this publication meets the minimum requirements
of the American National Standard for Permanence of Paper for Printed
Library Materials Z39.48-1984.

Bolton, S. Charles.
    Territorial ambition: land and society in Arkansas, 1800-1840 / S. Charles Bolton.
      p. cm.
    Includes bibliographical references and index.
    ISBN 1-55728-284-6
    1. Arkansas—History.   2. Arkansas—Economic conditions.
  I. Title.
  F411.B73   1993   92-39501
  976.7′03—dc20   CIP

In Memory of Mom and Dad, and Jeff

Author's Note

This is a reprint of the 1993 book with no changes to the text except to correct typographical errors. The only significant one of these is in Table 2, page 75, in which a transposition of numbers has been corrected and ratios adjusted. This edition also has a new index.

Acknowledgments

During the more than a decade in which I have been working on aspects of this book, a number of institutions and individuals have given me generous help for which I am very grateful. The University of Arkansas at Little Rock provided a semester of research time at the beginning of the project that allowed me to collect the original quantitative data; much later, another semester off gave me the opportunity to write a draft of the book. The staff of the Ottenheimer Library and especially its Archives and Special Collections have been unfailingly helpful and pleasant. The same is true of the people in Academic Computing Services. I have spent many hours at the State History Commission in Little Rock, my work there made easier by Archivist Russell Baker and the staff who handle microfilm and manuscripts. The National Archives in Washington, D.C., was also very helpful on both of my visits to that institution.

My friends and colleagues may well feel relieved to see this book in print. Vince Vinikas read all the chapters more than once, usually asking me to be a better historian than was my inclination and always improving my work. Harri Baker gave me much encouragement and a careful critique of the final draft. Carl Moneyhon, Frances Ross, and Fred Williams shared their considerable knowledge of Arkansas history and listened to my own anecdotes with indulgence. Stephen Recken provided warm encouragement and sage advice, often while running or riding a bicycle. Gerry Hanson's map-making skills and generosity I have exploited. David Sloan and Elliot West of the University of Arkansas, Fayetteville, have also been very helpful to me.

I also wish to thank the Arkansas Historical Association for permission to use portions of S. Charles Bolton, "Inequality on the Southern Frontier: Arkansas County in the Arkansas Territory," *Arkansas Historical Quarterly* 41 (Spring 1982): 51–66, and the *Journal of Interdisciplinary History* for similar use of S. Charles Bolton, "Economic Inequality in the Arkansas Territory," 14 (Winter 1984): 619–33, copyright 1984 by the Massachusetts Institute of Technology and the editors of *The Journal of Interdisciplinary History.*

Contents

Tables

Figures

Introduction

Territorial Arkansas has been most frequently symbolized in the Arkansas Traveler, that charming tale that has as its central figure a squatter who is canny and witty but hopelessly improvident. In Edward P. Washburn's famous depiction of the scene, the squatter sits on a barrel in his coonskin cap, holding a fiddle as he talks to the well-dressed traveler astride a fine horse. The squatter's home is a badly shingled, doorless cabin, decorated with an animal pelt and a misspelled sign indicating that whiskey is for sale; his wife smokes a corncob pipe while she, five children, and a lounging dog listen to the conversation. A memorable portion of the dialogue is the squatter's assertion that he hasn't repaired the roof because the job is impossible in the rain and unnecessary in dry weather.[1]

Unknown to most beholders of this powerful image is the fact that the traveler was not an eastern visitor but an Arkansan himself. Sandford Faulkner, who created the tale based on his own experience while electioneering in 1840, was a prominent planter and politician whose wealth and social graces made him as welcome in New Orleans as in Little Rock.[2] Thus, if the squatter demonstrates the existence of rural poverty and indolence in early Arkansas, then the traveler shows the presence of southern gentility. In reality, the poor-but-proud squatter of the Arkansas Traveler is a stereotype, displaying some characteristics of his society but exaggerating their importance.

If shiftlessness is associated with Arkansas Territory, so also is lawless-ness. Hiram Whittington, who had arrived in Arkansas from Massachusetts in 1827, chided his brother back home in Salem because the people there were "making a great fuss about the murder of one man." Whittington claimed that there had been twenty or thirty killings in Arkansas during the past year and only three murderers had been hanged. A few years later, George Featherstonhaugh, an English-born traveler, claimed that criminal-types were attracted to Arkansas and vice versa: "*Gentlemen* who had taken the liberty to imitate the signatures of other persons; *bankrupts* who were not disposed to be plundered by their creditors; *homicides, horse-stealers,* and *gamblers;* all admired Arkansas on account of the very gentle and tolerant state of public opinion which prevailed there in regard to such fundamental points as religion, morals, and property."[3]

Whittington and Featherstonhaugh both seem to have exaggerated for the sake of humor and probably also out of culture shock. Nonetheless, there is no reason to doubt the essence of what they wrote. Arkansas Territory was a violent place where duels occurred frequently, brawls were commonplace, and murder was something about which the average citizen might reasonably worry. Moreover, there was a significant population of counterfeiters, horse thieves, and other professional criminals.[4] In truth, both lawlessness and shiftlessness were important parts of Arkansas Territory. They are not, however, the whole story.

The following chapters examine Arkansas as an economic resource utilized by American society in the process of its expansion and self-definition in the early nineteenth century. This study begins with the arrival of the Spanish explorers and discusses both Native American and European colonial society, but it focuses on the activities of American pio-neers in the decades of the 1820s and 1830s when Arkansas Territory grew into statehood. The underlying hypothesis is that those Americans were ambitious to improve their lives in a material sense and that in large measure they succeeded. Arkansas Territory was more economically suc-cessful than the Arkansas Traveler would suggest or than historians have hitherto realized. It was a crude and sometimes brutal place, but it was also the scene of economic development as settlers moved from hunting and subsistence farming into market-oriented agriculture. The former quality has been exaggerated, and the latter largely has been ignored.

Not entirely ignored, one should add. Dissertations by Henry Ford White in 1931 and William Waddy Moore in 1962 discuss agricultural development in detail. Both of them, however, rely heavily on impression-istic evidence and make little attempt to assess the rate of economic change or its significance.[5] Perhaps for that reason, other historians have tended to discount the development of agriculture until the antebellum period and then to focus on the economic and political achievements of cotton planters. In these accounts, Arkansas Territory is populated by hunters and subsistence farmers, neither of which is given much credit for ambition. The territory was picturesque, it would seem, but not productive.[6] A recent study refers to the "economic doldrums" from which Arkansas emerged only in the 1850s, long after statehood in 1836.[7]

Historian Malcolm J. Rohrbough, whose knowledge of the early nineteenth-century frontier is magisterial, claims that "Arkansans hunted, trapped, grazed livestock, and generally pursued a lonely, solitary existence, consistent with their location in the most remote frontier of the West." Rohrbough is aware of agriculture. He discusses the development of cotton cultivation in the 1820s, the emergence of a planter class in the south and east beginning in the 1830s, and the presence of small farmers raising corn and livestock in the north and west. Still, assessing the economy in 1840, Rohrbough is most impressed by the small size of Arkansas's population, the continuing importance of hunting, and the settlers' alleged lack of enthusiasm for the hard work of farming.[8]

This negative view of economic progress in territorial Arkansas is strangely out of place with the westward movement of the American people in general. In his 1954 study, *People of Plenty*, David Potter argues that the American character has been shaped by economic abundance, that is, the possession of national wealth that was extreme in comparison with other countries. With respect to the early nineteenth century, Potter declares that "the major form in which abundance presented itself was the fertility of unsettled land." He agrees with Frederick Jackson Turner that the frontier had played a vital role in American development. Turner, however, had argued for a broad cultural transformation and the creation of a unique American society with its distinctive penchant for democracy. Potter believes the function of the frontier was more narrowly economic and that the role played by available land would later be fulfilled by other forms of economic opportunity.[9]

Potter sees economic abundance as having social and political significance. Following Alexis de Tocqueville, he claims that the American concept of equality involved equal access to opportunity rather than similarity of estate. Thus Americans had no wish to take from the rich in the interest of social leveling, but they did demand economic conditions that allowed a reasonable chance to improve one's economic status and a long shot at becoming rich. Political stability in the United States, according to

Potter, depended on the existence of that environment of opportunity. "Democracy made this promise [of equality] . . . and our democratic system . . . survived because an economic surplus was available to pay democracy's promissory note."[10] What, one wonders, was Arkansas's role in this?

In some respects this book is a test of the Potter thesis. It asks whether land was available in Arkansas Territory in a manner that supports the concept of economic abundance, whether that land was utilized successfully, and whether there was enough opportunity to fulfill the demands of equality as Americans understood it. This emphasis on ownership of the soil is supported by historian Robert Wiebe's recent assertion that land was "still the ultimate objective for most Americans" of the Jacksonian era. This study also pursues other issues related to the nature of society in Jacksonian America, those frenzied three decades of economic change and social fermentation between the War of 1812 and the Mexican War. How did American settlers in Arkansas organize themselves into a social structure? What degree of economic inequality existed in Arkansas Territory and what element of social class? How much economic and social mobility was present? How were the economic interests of the settlers expressed by their political system?[11]

Diverse interests and motivations brought people to Arkansas Territory, and various geographical impediments limited their numbers. Still, the principal goal of the settlers who did come was to own land and produce agricultural commodities in the hope of making a better life for themselves. To a significant degree, they fulfilled this aspiration, a truth attested to by land records, tax assessments, and the agricultural data in the United States Census of 1840. There was a significant degree of economic growth in Arkansas Territory—more land, slaves, and livestock per taxpayer over time—and by 1840 per-capita production of agricultural products compared favorably with nearby states. A slave-owning, cotton-producing society in the lowland south and east was geographically balanced by an economy of smaller scale and more diversified farms in the highland north and west. The distribution of wealth in both sections was very unequal, but a lowland planter class stood out from the mass of yeomen farmers. Social mobility was high: some men took advantage of economic and political opportunity to raise their status, while others were overturned by misfortune or folly and fell back.

Arkansas Territory was a competitive environment, a fact suggested by its economic growth and pronounced inequality and illustrated in the sharp and sometimes lawless struggle for land and the ruthless and occasionally bloody quests for political office. As they sought advancement for themselves, territorial citizens believed they were furthering the national interest; they expected help from the federal government and often received it. Their viewpoint was consistent with Jeffersonian political economy as defined by historian Joyce Appleby: "a commitment to growth through the unimpeded exertions of individuals whose access to economic opportunity was both protected and facilitated by government."[12]

Yet it is not clear that all Arkansans were market-oriented capitalists. The most common unit of economic output was the family farm, run by a family that in some ways resembled that of the colonial period and which produced prodigious amounts of corn and pork. It seems reasonable to assume that subsistence was its major goal and that commodity exchange or sale was a secondary consideration. It may be that the herders, squatters, and small landowners of Arkansas had no sympathy for the market orientation of the cotton planters or for the emphasis on economic development that was voiced by the newspapers and the legislature of the territory. A detailed examination of that issue must await another study. The evidence here indicates that the settlement of Arkansas was part and parcel of the advancing market economy of the United States; it does not make clear the extent to which all groups participated in the transformation.[13]

Arkansas was a "new country," in the phrase of the time. To most Americans of the early republic that meant fertile and inexpensive land, political offices as yet unfilled, and a social structure with openings at the top. To some, of course, "new country" meant forests in which to hunt and live in isolation and independence, and perhaps a place in which to hide from the law. Hunters, subsistence farmers, herders, and desperadoes were all a part of Arkansas Territory. Most settlers, however, came there to get more and richer land than they had and build better lives for themselves and their families. Among them were a few restless men of larger hopes whose impatient desire for rapid and high advancement was an extreme form of ambition, the signature characteristic of the "Era of the Common Man."[14] Collectively, these white men and women pushed aside Native Americans and exploited African Americans in order to create an agricultural economy and a social and political order that would satisfy their own ambitions. Their story is not always pretty, but it is usually interesting.

one

Clearing the Land

Long before its American settlement, what is now Arkansas was an object of European ambition, and it was visited by two explorers who were major figures in the imperial activities of their respective countries. Hernando de Soto traversed the area with an army in 1541 in a quest for precious metals and personal dominion under the flag of Spain, and René-Robert Cavelier de Sieur la Salle stopped briefly at the mouth of the Arkansas River in 1682 while attempting to create a vast inland fur-trading empire for France. Eventually the French effort resulted in a small European settlement centered at Arkansas Post, which maintained its existence down to the arrival of the Americans. This decidedly unspectacular colonization was dwarfed in significance by the effect of European germs on the Native Americans. American settlers felled trees in Arkansas in the nineteenth century, but the Spaniards and the French had already cleared the land in a more effective manner by communicating deadly diseases to the Indians.

~

The idea that the settlement of the United States involved the taming of a wilderness is central to the national mythology of the country and to the cultural identity of Americans.[1] It ignores, however, the fact that the New World was neither uninhabited nor uncultivated, and it discounts the existence and the accomplishments of Native Americans. Transplanted Europeans believed that the peoples they knew as Indians were few in number and manifestly savage, that they embellished the wilderness without changing its essential character.[2] Comforting as it was for the pioneer to belittle the people whose land he wanted, the evidence requires a different judgment from us. Historian Francis Jennings provides an accurate and pithy revision of the myth of virgin land: "European explorers and invaders discovered an inhabited land . . . and displaced a resident population."[3]

The New World was heavily populated when Columbus arrived, but it did not long remain so. The exact numbers are a matter of controversy, and the truth will never be known precisely, but it is possible to make a reasonable estimate by beginning with the size of tribal populations at their nadir, applying rates of decline that seem supported by the evidence, and making mathematical projections into the past. A recent estimate of this type by Russell Thornton indicates there were some 92 million people living in the Western Hemisphere in 1492 and that 5.6 million of them made their homes within the borders of the present United States.[4] North America was much less crowded than South America, but the area of the United States still contained more people in 1492 than it did when Thomas Jefferson became president.

The rapid decline of these aborigines resulted from the introduction of Old World diseases such as smallpox, typhus, and measels. Unwittingly, the Europeans passed on their illnesses to the Indians, who lacked immunities to these alien organisms, and the outcome was a demographic catastrophe. Within a century of Cortes's invasion of central Mexico, the native population had dropped from 25 million to 2 million. In North America, the Hurons of Canada were reduced from 32,000 people to 10,000 during 10 years of the early seventeenth century. The Pequots of New England had boasted 4,000 warriors before the English arrived, but sickness and war reduced them to 300 fighting men in 1674. The land often did seem nearly uninhabited to its new settlers, but its wildness was newly created by the mortality of the Indians. As Jennings has written, "the American land was more like a widow than a virgin."[5]

The concept of land cleared of its original inhabitants and resettled by newcomers applies nicely to Arkansas. Five hundred years ago, when Columbus made his fateful landfall, a horticultural and urbanized society existed in northeast Arkansas between Crowley's Ridge and the Mississippi River, and similar but less-concentrated population centers were located on all the major rivers of the present state. The number of people associated with this aboriginal culture is a matter of some dispute. Thornton's estimate of 5.6 million Indians in what is now the United States yields an average of 1.9 per square mile, which would give Arkansas about 100,000 persons.

Henry Dobyns, however, has estimated that the Mississippi River Valley and the river basins flowing into it could have supported a population of 6.55 native inhabitants per square mile, which would give the present state of Arkansas a population of just under 350,000. A much lower estimate comes from Dan F. and Phyllis A. Morse, archeologists and experts on the protohistoric sites in Arkansas, who argue that there were some 150 major population centers with an average of about 500 inhabitants each. Thus, assert the Morses, "for now, we can assume a maximum population of about 75,000."[6] Recognizing that we do not have a definitive answer, we shall accept the figure of 75,000 inhabitants in Arkansas prior to European contact on the grounds that it has the strongest empirical basis. Let us now see what happened to these people.

The first historical evidence of Arkansas and its population comes from the expedition led by Hernando de Soto, which followed the Spanish conquest of Mexico and Peru. De Soto himself had been a lieutenant of Pizarro in Peru and had participated in the treacherous ambush that resulted in the capture of Atahualpa, the Inca king. Enriched by that adventure, he remained ambitious even by conquistadorial standards. The object of his North American expedition was to conquer all the territory between Florida and Mexico, somewhere in the inland of which he hoped to find an Indian empire of Inca-like wealth. Charles V, Holy Roman emperor and king of Spain, gave official approval to the expedition and expected half of all the bullion seized and title to the conquered lands. De Soto and his men provided their own funding, in anticipation of the great wealth that was to follow. The king also appointed de Soto governor-general of the anticipated new dominion.[7]

Starting at Tampa Bay, Florida, in June of 1539, the Spaniards marched, fought, and plundered their way as far north as South Carolina and as far west as Texas, never finding the precious metals they sought and always exhibiting that combination of intense fortitude and cruelty that marked conquistadorial behavior. The expedition spent nearly two years in Arkansas amidst the extensive and well-provisioned aboriginal population. The findings of the De Soto Commission in 1939, which mapped de Soto's route in Arkansas by reconciling Spanish texts with contemporary geography, have been supplanted recently by a group of modern scholars, led by Charles Hudson, whose knowledge of Native American habitations is enriched by the findings of recent archeological work.[8] The newer interpretation is followed below.

The first contact between de Soto and the Arkansas Indians took place in June 1541 as the Spaniards prepared to cross the Mississippi River, some twenty miles below modern Memphis. The anonymous "Gentleman of Elvas," who wrote the most detailed among the three "eyewitness" accounts of the de Soto expedition, described the two hundred dugout canoes filled with bowmen who came from the western shore to harass the Spanish expedition. The warriors "were painted with ochre, wearing great bunches of white and other plumes of many colours, having feathered shields in their hands," and the chiefs sat in vessels fitted with canopies or awnings. "With the awnings, the plumes, and the shields, the pennons, and the number of people in the fleet, it appeared like a famous armada of galleys." Rodrigo Ranjel, de Soto's private secretary, estimated there were seven thousand persons in the two hundred canoes, apparently having decided that each vessel held about thirty-five individuals.[9]

Several weeks later, the de Soto expedition arrived at Pacaha, a town on the Mississippi River to the north of where the Spaniards had crossed. It was, says the Gentleman of Elvas, "enclosed and very large. In the towers and the palisade were many loopholes . . . [from] a great lake near to the enclosure . . . water entered a ditch that well-nigh went round the town. From the River Grande [Mississippi] was a canal." The people of Pacaha fled from de Soto, who had allied with their enemies, and took refuge on an island in the Mississippi River. At that place, the Spaniards estimated their numbers at "five or six thousand souls."[10]

This portion of northeast Arkansas was very heavily populated. Near Pacaha there were other "large towns" within a few miles. Ranjel speaks of Pacaha and nearby Aquixo and Casqui as "the best villages seen up to that time, better stockaded and fortified." The Gentleman of Elvas and Hernandez de Biedma, the king of Spain's representative on the expedition, agree that the town of Quiguate, in the same region, was the largest urban area encountered by the Spaniards on their conquest.[11]

Arkansas was not only inhabited but also cultivated in the sixteenth century. At Pacaha the Spaniards found "much dry maize," a phrase that becomes meaningful when we consider that the expedition numbered more than three hundred Spanish soldiers as well as a large retinue of Indian slaves and concubines. De Soto had lost his supplies during an Indian attack in Alabama and had little food except for his herd of pigs. He remained at Pacaha for nearly a month, presumably filling up on corn and on the abundant fish in the canal that were easily caught with nets. When they moved inland, the Spaniards were able to plunder and extort more food. Rodrigo Ranjel tells us that the Spaniards "took much people and clothes, and a vast amount of provisions and much salt" from the central Arkansas town of Coligua. During the winter of 1541–42, the expedition rested at Autiamque, on the Arkansas River below present-day Little Rock. The inhabitants had fled, and the Spaniards found "maize, beans" and wild foods in "greatest plenty."[12]

Garcilaso de la Vega, whose narrative is based on the recollections of an expedition survivor taken down some forty years later, claims that at Autiamque the conquistadores "passed the best of all winters they experienced in Florida." Despite heavy snowfalls that kept them in for a month and a half and the Indian skirmishes that accompanied their hunting trips, "they could not have been more comfortable or even so comfortable in the dwellings of their families in Spain."[13]

We have no record of what occurred in Arkansas between 1542 or 1543, when the Spaniards left, and 1673, when the small party led by French explorer Louis Jolliet and including Jesuit Father Jacques Marquette paddled down the Mississippi River to an Indian village known as "Arkcansea" that provided a name for the Arkansas River near whose mouth it was located. The Quapaws, as the inhabitants came to be called, may have numbered six thousand when the French first visited them, and they were skilled farmers and potters as well as hunters and warriors. They were almost the only inhabitants of eastern Arkansas, however, and they lacked the complex population centers found by the Spaniards. The French would later encounter Caddos on the Red River, Cahinnio Indians on the Ouachita River, and small groups of Tunica and Korea Indians in the southeastern part of the state, but nowhere did they find or hear of Indian societies on the scale of those described in the de Soto narratives.[14]

The best explanation for the drastic decline in the numbers of Indians in Arkansas is that the de Soto expedition unknowingly created an epidemiological disaster by transferring European disease germs to the natives. In addition to their lack of immunity to European germs and viruses, the concentrated villages of the aborigineal population would have increased their mortality rates.[15] Population decline and cultural change make it difficult to identify positively any seventeenth-century Arkansas Indians as descendents of those who flourished in the sixteenth century. The Quapaw may represent the remnants of the people de Soto knew in eastern Arkansas; on the other hand, they may have migrated from the Ohio River region in the early seventeenth century, taking advantage of the fact that the previous occupants of the area were largely gone. The Caddos and their relatives, who lived on the Red and Ouachita rivers in the seventeenth century, were probably descendents of the Cayas, who fought bravely against the Spaniards. In any case, a century and a half after the Spanish invasion of Arkansas, the Indians' population was greatly reduced, probably to fewer than 15,000.[16]

The Quapaws soon suffered a fate that seems to provide a model for the decline of their predecessors. In 1682, Henri de Tonti estimated that the four Quapaw villages contained no more than 1,500 warriors, by which he probably meant able-bodied, adult males. In 1699, three French priests from Quebec visited the Quapaws and noted the devastating effects of a recent smallpox epidemic. Because of the high mortality, the tribe had consolidated its villages into two, and the priests estimated that there were only 300 warriors. A quarter of a century of contact with the French, who were their friends, had reduced the Quapaw nation, it would seem, by about 80 percent.[17]

$\sim$

Despite its devastating consequences, the European occupation of Arkansas was never extensive. Jolliet's exploration was intended to extend French dominion from the Great Lakes south to the Gulf of Mexico, thereby thwarting both Spain and England. The effort was successful, but imperial power lay lightly. The ambitious La Salle, who sung a hymn at the mouth of the Mississippi River in the spring of 1682 and claimed its entire valley in the name of Louis XIV of France, was as relentlessly goal-oriented as any conquistador, but he dreamed of profit rather than of booty, of furs and skins rather than of gold and silver.[18] Unlike the Spaniards, the French sought a commercial relationship with the Indians, who would need both their lives and freedom in order to uphold their end of the relationship. Nor were the French driven by the population pressures that were pushing the English colonists toward the west, wresting land from the Indians as they went. Indeed, the French empire in the New World contained very few Frenchmen, and Arkansas would get only a handful of them.

La Salle had visited the Quapaws on his way from Canada to the mouth of the Mississippi. Henri de Tonti, his lieutenant, founded Arkansas Post in 1686 when he left six men at the Quapaw village near Little Prairie, some twenty-seven miles up the Arkansas River, in the hope that they would begin a profitable trade with the Indians.[19] The following year Henri Joutel and his companions arrived on the south bank of the Arkansas River, having trekked all the way from Matagorda Bay in Texas, where La Salle's final expedition had ended in disaster and in the death of its leader. Joutel rejoiced to see Arkansas Post on the other side of the river, "a great Cross, and at a small Distance from it, a House, built after the French Fashion."[20]

Tonti's post, however, did not flourish. The Quapaws, who were to supply the furs and skins, were greatly weakened by their illnesses, and the beaver of the Arkansas River, which had excited the interest of the French, proved to be few in number and inferior in quality to those of the North. Warfare encouraged by the imperial conflict between France and England made it more difficult to reach Montreal, and the merchants there preferred to deal with Indians directly in any case. Even by Joutel's arrival, four of the six original traders had left the post. Within a decade all were gone, and in 1701 Tonti lost his legal claim to the operation.[21]

Arkansas seems to have had no permanent European residents in the eighteenth century until John Law's colonists arrived in 1721. Law was a Scottish financier who had gained great influence in France, and who created the Compagnie d'Occident in 1717 and won for it a monopoly over the trade of Louisiana. To sell shares in his company, Law utilized a shameless publicity campaign that pictured gold, silver, pearls, and emeralds as important natural resources of Louisiana. As the stock went up, Law merged the company with others and tied their collective stock to the public finances of France. Speculation increased, creating the Mississippi Bubble, which eventually burst, bankrupting Law and many innocent investors. In August of 1721, after Law had fled France, a group of company settlers, numbering as many as eighty, arrived in Arkansas and began to make homes near Tonti's now extinct post.

Law had conceived Arkansas as an agricultural colony that would also serve as a way station for boats traveling from New Orleans to Kaskaskia in the Illinois Country. His colonists seem to have done their best but to little avail. They lived on the edge of a prairie, but their plows could not penetrate its tough sod. After a year they managed to clear and cultivate two and a half acres. Their best agricultural success came in planting widowed land, fields that had been abandoned by the Quapaw. As the Compagnie d'Occident ceased to be active, the population of the colony declined. In 1722, there were fifty colonists and eighteen soldiers at the rejuvenated post. By 1727, however, the soldiers had been withdrawn and there were only thirty Frenchmen.[22]

Louisiana again became a colony of the French Crown in 1731 and that produced some activity at Arkansas Post. Twelve soldiers were stationed there, and by 1734 the post included a house for the commandant, a barracks, a powder magazine, and a jail. Despite this military presence, however, a Chickasaw attack in 1749 killed six men and carried off eight women and children.[23] After that event, Arkansas Post was moved from its original location, some twenty-seven miles from the mouth of the Mississippi, to a place called *Écores Rouges,* which was another nine miles upstream. The new location was less prone to flooding, but it was also very inconvenient to

Mississippi River traffic. Thus, in 1756, the post was moved again, this time to a site about ten miles from the mouth of the Mississippi.[24]

By the middle of the eighteenth century, Arkansas Post was a small military outpost, a center for hunting and trading, and a tiny agricultural village. A census of the civilian population taken sometime in 1749 illustrates the economic character of the community. Seven French families and fourteen slaves, forty-five people in all, resided at the post. Charles Linctot, a native of Quebec, was the principal slaveholder with seven bondsmen. Collectively, these *habitants* owned twenty-nine oxen, suggesting a significant amount of agricultural activity. In addition there were three horses, sixty cows, and twenty-nine pigs. The preponderant influence of hunting and trading, however, is indicated by the presence of sixty-five *voyageurs*, "who live as much on the River as at the Post . . ." There were forty of these on the Arkansas River, eleven *bourgeois*, who worked for themselves, and twenty-nine *engages*, or hired men. An additional five *voyageurs* were working the White River, and four were on the St. Francis River. Sixteen more were in Arkansas Post "to Equip Themselves to Return to the Hunt." The number of French troops usually at the post was probably well under the thirty-one who were enumerated in September 1763.[25]

Lt. Philip Pittman of the British army visited the post in 1765. He described a fort consisting of five buildings surrounded by a stockade one hundred and eighty feet in length in which were set a number of three-pound cannon. Everything, however, according to Pittman, "was in ruinous condition." There were eight families of farmers, and they had cleared the land nine hundred yards back from the river, but because of the sandy soil and the frequent flooding, "they do not raise their necessary provisions." The economic subsistence of the post, according to Pittman, was hunting, and the products that went to New Orleans were "great quantities of bear's oil, tallow, salted buffaloe meat, and a few skins."[26]

Meanwhile, the Quapaws remained faithful allies of the French but continued to diminish in numbers. Quapaw warriors fought a number of battles, alone and with French allies, against the Chickasaws, who were supporters of the English. Le Page du Pratz, the contemporary historian of Louisiana, said that they were "no less distinguished for being good hunters than stout warriors." Pittman claimed that they were "reckoned amongst the bravest of the southern Indians." Their culture had changed however. They farmed less and hunted more in order to pay for the European goods on which they were increasingly dependent. Alcoholism was a growing problem. Disease was less devastating, but along with warfare it led to a continual loss of population. A census conducted by the

Spaniards in 1777 revealed only 509 Quapaws, 176 of whom were "warriors," that is, males over twelve years.[27]

The character of Arkansas Post changed very little as a result of the Treaty of Paris in 1763, which gave Louisiana to Spain. Flooding was a major problem at the new location, only ten miles from the Mississippi River, prompting one inundated commandant to describe his post as "the most disagreeable hole in the universe." This was finally remedied, or at least improved, in 1779, when the Spaniards removed the post to its previous location on *Écore Rouges,* thirty-six miles from the mouth of the Arkansas. In the manner of the French, the Spaniards usually allowed the fortifications of what they called Fort Carlos III to lapse into decay. They improved them somewhat, however, after 1781, when Spain entered the War of American Independence. A reward for this military preparedness came in 1783, when Captain Jacobo Dubrueil and the garrison of Fort Carlos III fought off an attack by the Tory partisan leader James Colbert. Dubrueil's victory won him a promotion, and it gave Arkansas a small but successful role in the American Revolution.[28]

Much less effective was the Spanish attempt to deal with the Osage Indians, who lived in western Missouri but spent much time in Arkansas during the latter part of the eighteenth century. The Osages were hunters, horsemen, and fierce fighters who ranged widely on the Spanish frontier, trading at St. Louis and stealing horses from the Caddo, and who were under the protection of the Spanish post at Natchitoches on the Red River; the Osages also hunted in the Arkansas River Valley, where they occasionally robbed and killed a white hunter.[29]

Athanase de Mézières, the commandant at Natchitoches, blamed the Arkansas hunters for an increase in Osage violence that occurred in 1770. According to de Mézières, the Arkansas River was "the asylum of the most wicked persons," deserters and thieves who had lived away from "Christian lands" for decades and who used Indian women as slaves and prostitutes. He claimed that these men had illegally furnished the Osages with weapons and incited them to raid "this district" for Indian children and horses. Whatever the truth of that claim, the Osages also posed a threat to the livelihood of Arkansas Post, having increased their assaults on its hunters and traders. In 1772 there was reason to believe that Osage war parties would attack the garrison itself. No such confrontation took place, but Quapaw warriors took five Osage scalps in 1773, and sporadic violence continued for the rest of the century. In 1800, the commandant of Natchitoches wrote that "there is no year in which these cursed Osages do not kill some of the hunters either of this post or of Arkansas Post."[30]

The Osage problem was caused by the weakness of Spanish authority. Traders from the Arkansas Post apparently did trade illegally with the Osages; on the other hand, Spain was simply unable to deal with the eight hundred Osage warriors in a forceful manner. Moreover, the Osages brought more deerskins to St. Louis than did any other tribe, and the merchants there did not want the government to take punitive action that would upset their business. Lack of power meant that the interests of one district were balanced against those of another, and the undeveloped nature of Arkansas Post counted against it. In St. Louis in 1797, the lieutenant governor of Upper Louisiana, Zenon Trudeau, argued for leniency toward the Osages because the "farmers of these establishments . . . [are] more important than the few hunters of the Arkansas River."[31]

Trudeau exaggerated the wild character of Arkansas, but not by much. As late as 1791, the civilian population of Arkansas Post numbered only 151 persons, including 37 slaves. The census of that year identifies 27 households, 18 of which were headed by farmers, 5 by merchants, 2 by seamstresses, 1 by a carpenter, and 1 by an artisan. The two largest slaveholders were the Widow Menard, who owned 9 slaves and was listed as a merchant, and the Widow "Deruisseaux," a farmer, who owned 8. Joseph Bogy, another farmer, had the largest household, which included 7 slaves and 4 hired men. Five households were headed by women. Deruisseaux, Menard, and the Widow Dianne, a merchant, were listed by their surnames. The 2 seamstresses were listed as "Jeanne" and "Mariana," and it was noted that they were part Indian. Among the 106 white inhabitants of the post, 41 were children, probably 12 years and under. The adults, or at least those 13 and over, included 41 males and only 24 females. The census makes no mention of the hunters, who apparently were not considered residents, but they would have swelled the population by perhaps 100 persons.[32]

At Ste. Genevieve, a community of French settlers just below St. Louis, the farmers cultivated private strips in one large field that lay along the Mississippi River, following the custom in northern France and in Canada. Oxen rather than horses pulled the plows, slaves and day laborers supplemented the efforts of the landowners, and the principal crops were wheat, corn, and tobacco. Agricultural activity at Arkansas Post seems to have been similar. Philip Pittman commented in 1765 that the farmers at Arkansas Post "had cleared the land about nine hundred yards in depth," suggesting that they too were working a single field.[33] As we have seen, in 1749, the post contained 29 oxen and only 3 horses. Arkansas Post also used the same type of human work force as Ste. Genevieve and produced the same products. There was a difference, however: Ste. Genevieve was a farming village while Arkansas Post was a trading center frequented by Indians and white hunters where farming was incidental rather than central to the economy. Morris S. Arnold, the premier historian of French Arkansas, believes "there were never more than eight or ten real farmers" at Arkansas Post.[34]

The population of Arkansas Post increased during the 1790s, but agricultural production fell off after a strong showing in 1793. In that year there were 220 people organized into 40 households, 27 of which were producing at least some wheat, corn, or tobacco. Their output of cereal grain amounted to about 18 minots, or large bushels, of corn for each resident and about 8 minots of wheat. This would have more than enough to meet the needs of subsistence. In the remaining 3 years for which we have records, 1794, 1796, and 1798, agricultural production fell off despite a swelling population. In 1798 there were 393 residents at the post, but they managed to raise only 2 minots of wheat and 3 minots of corn per inhabitant, probably not enough for subsistence. Had they been sold rather than consumed, the commodities produced at Arkansas Post would not have been worth a great deal. Morris S. Arnold estimates the average annual value of production during the 1790s at only $4,822, with wheat accounting for $2,132, corn for $2,410, and tobacco for $280.

The population growth of the 1790s included the first trickle of American settlers. The largest jump occurred between 1793 and 1794 and may have involved the counting of hunters as part of the resident population. Nonetheless, there were 8 or 10 American families at the post in 1798, some of whom were newly arrived. Most of the new residents were not slaveholders. The 37 slaves of 1791 had grown to 56 in 1798, but had dropped from 25 percent of the total population to 14 percent. The growth was not very disruptive. At least 75 percent of the population in 1798 were French, and the two leading agricultural producers were Joseph Bogy and the Widow Deruisseaux, who were the leading agricultural producers for a decade.[35]

~

In October of 1800, Arkansas once again fell within the focus of a European ambition as Napolean forced Spain to return Louisiana to France so that he might create a new North American empire. President Thomas Jefferson was ready to ally the United States with Great Britain if the French plan succeeded. It did not, of course, and instead the Louisiana Purchase allowed Jefferson to double the size of his country at a cost of only fifteen million dollars and some scruples about not exercising powers that were only implied in the Constitution. Louisiana, the western watershed of the Mississippi River, became officially a part of the United States on December 20, 1803.

A description of Arkansas as it emerged from its colonial period under Spain and France was provided by John B. Treat, who arrived at Arkansas Post around the first of September 1805 to establish a United States government factory or trading post. Treat found sixty to seventy families living at Arkansas Post or in the vicinity and another seven or eight families located farther up the Arkansas River. Among these European and American settlers were sixty blacks, almost all of them slaves, making a total of perhaps five hundred people. Native Americans were not much more numerous. Treat believed the Quapaws had fewer than three hundred "warriors or Gun Men," an overestimate that probably included a village of Choctaws who had intermarried with the Quapaws and lived near them. "No other Indians are found residing on the Arkansas [River] thoughout its whole extent," nor was Treat aware of any other Indians in what is now the state of Arkansas except for occasional Osage hunting parties. Assuming there were three hundred adult male Native Americans living on the lower Arkansas, they probably represented a total population of well under nine hundred people. Thus the population of Arkansas had dropped from seventy-five thousand or more when de Soto arrived to fifteen hundred or less when the Americans took control of the area.[36]

Agriculture was "in its Infancy" at Arkansas Post, according to Treat, but some settlers were working hard at it, particularly six families recently arrived from the United States. Treat did not think the land was as fertile as that in the Ohio River Valley, but it was producing in a very respectable manner. Wheat, hemp, flax, corn, and cotton grew well even where the land had been cultivated for up to ten years. Treat claimed that the settlers were giving up corn because it was eaten by crows and black birds—a curious comment in light of the later agricultural history of Arkansas! Cotton was raised by everybody "for domestic purposes . . . and there are instances of several Acres having been cultivated upon separate Plantations." The absence of a cotton gin held back further developments.

Cattle, sheep, and hogs were numerous at Arkansas Post. Especially the first two, said Treat, and this, too, is surprising when one considers the future success of pork in Arkansas. Arkansas livestock was as good as any in the United States, but Treat gave little credit to the settlers, "for nature having made such ample provision, that man makes no trouble about them." Mild winters allowed the livestock "a bountiful supply of Cane," and the large and fertile prairies gave them pasture the rest of the year, "large numbers of Cattle are to be seen grazing here." Treat was lyrical about the prairie near Arkansas Post, which "affords (when in yellow bloom) a scene as perhaps not to be excell'd in nature" and one where "we behold Nature in her most varied and beautiful attire" all summer and into the fall as "flowers had the appearance of shooting forth to change the scene."[37]

Arkansas came to the United States largely devoid of people but with its agricultural potential intact. The populous towns and fruitful fields of de Soto's time were long gone, the Indians of that culture having fallen victim both to Spanish steel and Old World pestilence. The brave and true Quapaws were mostly gone also, succumbing to smallpox and alcoholism, and to the warfare they undertook in the service of France and Spain. Replacing these aborigines, western civilization had provided a single village, a few outlying farms, and several score of hunters. A sad tale perhaps, but one that meant opportunity to the Americans who now looked at Arkansas from across the river as de Soto once had done.

two

Settlers, Real and Mythic

Americans moved across the Mississippi River after the Louisiana Purchase, but they were slow to enter the future state of Arkansas. Between 1810 and 1820, however, a significant migration out of Missouri settled the interior portions of Arkansas and provided a basis for the organization of the area as a separate territory in 1819. The rate of growth slowed in the next decade, partly because the United States government continued to think of Arkansas Territory as a domicile for Native Americans removed from the East. In the 1830s, however, Arkansas grew rapidly along with the rest of the American frontier. It became a state in 1836 and boasted nearly a hundred thousand people by 1840. Still, Arkansas remained a frontier with fewer than two citizens per square mile and with a western border on the Indian Territory. Travelers and even local writers described the people of Arkansas as crude, violent, lawless, and lacking in industry, creating an enduring image. When closely examined, however, these same sources support a different interpretation, one that makes Arkansas more ordinary than bizarre and more cultivated than wild.

~

For a decade or so, Arkansas Post remained the center of activity in Arkansas. In 1805, as we have seen, the settlers and their slaves numbered about 500 people. Five years later, the United States Census of 1810 listed 188 persons at "Settlements of Hopefield [present-day West Memphis] and St. Francis," and 874 persons at "Settlements on the Arkansas."

Historians have generally accepted the total of these, 1,062, as the population of Arkansas in 1810.[1] In 1814 the white males of Arkansas were counted to apportion seats in the legislature of Missouri Territory. The 827 white males enumerated were 50 percent more than appeared on the census of 1810 and must have represented a population of about 1,588 people.[2] Eastern Arkansas was beginning to grow before the War of 1812, but a more important growth was taking place in the interior.

In fact, both the census of 1810 and the apportionment count of 1814 are probably inadequate because they represent the view from Arkansas Post and fail to count new settlers in the northeast and southwest. By the time these enumerations were made, people were moving into Arkansas overland from what is now the state of Missouri, which had swelled in population from about 6,000 in 1800 to about 19,000 in 1810. As southeastern Missouri began to fill up, pioneers migrated down the Southwest Trail that began at Ste. Genevieve and entered Arkansas across the Current River in what is now Randolph County, making new homes in the river valleys of northeast Arkansas.[3] Later settlers went farther down the trail, moving in a southwesterly direction, crossing the Arkansas River in the vicinity of present-day Little Rock, and continuing on as far as the Red River. Little Rock is about 100 river miles from Arkansas Post, and any other point on the Southwest Trail is farther away. These settlers were almost certainly not counted in 1810 or in 1814, yet they were the basis for the new American society that would develop in Arkansas. (See figure 1.)

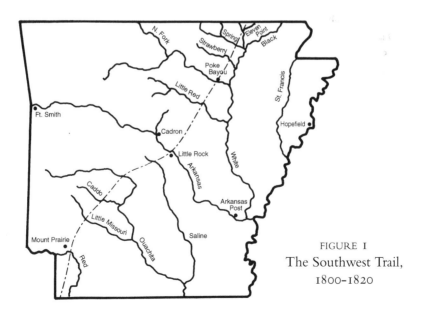

FIGURE I

The Southwest Trail,
1800–1820

An early report of what was taking place comes in a description of public lands in Missouri Territory written in April of 1814 by William Russell, a surveyor and land speculator based in St. Louis. Russell noted the scattered settlements located along the Current, Eleven Point, and Spring rivers, all of which flow out of what is now Missouri south toward the White River of Arkansas, and along the Strawberry River in the same area. He emphasized the "considerable quantity of rich and valuable Lands on White River" and the existence of "quite a promising (young) settlement at Poke Bayou," the site of modern Batesville.[4]

A more elaborate description of "Arkansas country" in 1814 comes from William Stevenson, a Methodist clergyman living in Potosi, Missouri, who visited his brother's farm on the Ouachita River. On his long journey down the Southwest Trail, Stevenson found "mostly wilderness except on the rivers and rich lands," where there were "settlements of industrious people" as well as "many hunters for wild game." He noted the existence of "growing and promising settlements" on the White, Spring, and Current rivers in northeast Arkansas, and he found similar pockets of immigration in the southwest, all the way to the Red River. On the Ouachita River and along smaller streams in the vicinity of modern Arkadelphia, he found "a great many small settlements all through the country from five to twenty miles apart." These settlers had brought their belongings on packhorses because there were no wagon roads and few ferries.[5]

The migration from Missouri into Arkansas seems to have begun about 1810. There were at least a few settlers in northeast Arkansas in that year. Most of the early settlers on the Arkansas River in the vicinity of Little Rock came up the river from Arkansas Post, but some were from Missouri and might have come down the Southwest Trail. Col. Alexander McFarland, a hunter and trader who settled at Cadron in 1808, was one of the latter. The earliest date for a large migration came from a group of some two hundred families living in the region between the Ouachita River and the Red River who reported to Missouri Governor William Clark in 1816 that they had arrived in what was then "a wilderness country ... about four years ago."[6] If, as this indicates, there were some one thousand people at the lower end of the Southwest Trail by the end of 1812, then it is very likely that larger numbers of people were living at the upper end of the trail and had arrived earlier. The specific nature of the census of 1810, which listed the communities that were counted, also suggests that the enumerator was aware of other centers of population that were uncounted. It is impossible to know the actual population of Arkansas in 1810, but the census of that year is certainly too low.

The significance of the migration from Missouri can be appreciated by looking at the pattern of growth in civil government in Arkansas. In 1804, Congress divided the Louisiana Purchase at the 33d parallel, the present southern boundary of Arkansas, and created a Territory of Orleans in the south with its capital at New Orleans and a District of Louisiana in the north, which was placed under the control of the territorial government of Indiana. The following year the District of Louisiana became the Territory of Louisiana with its capital at St. Louis. The Arkansas Post area was at first part of the New Madrid District, the southernmost jurisdiction of the Territory of Louisiana.

The isolation of Arkansas Post from St. Louis, or even from New Madrid, suggested that it should have some local autonomy, but its lack of population worked against an independent status. The St. Louis government created an Arkansas District in 1806, eliminated it in 1807, and recreated it in 1808. Local courts began to operate at the post in 1808 and continued in a desultory fashion for several years. Perhaps half of the thousand or so settlers spoke only French and had little familiarity with or interest in American jurisprudence. In 1812, when the Territory of Orleans entered the Union as the state of Louisiana, the Territory of Louisiana became the Territory of Missouri. In 1813 Arkansas became a separate county within the Missouri Territory.[7]

The population growth that was taking place along the Southwest Trail must have become apparent to the legislature of Missouri Territory by 1815. That year, the legislature divided Arkansas County, which had covered all of present Arkansas, to create Lawrence County, which encompassed the northern third of the area, including the White River region. In 1818 the St. Louis government added three more counties: Clark County in the Ouachita River area of south Arkansas; Hempstead County, which ran west of there to the Red River; and Pulaski County, which covered the Arkansas River in the central part of Arkansas. In 1820 the legislature of the newly created Arkansas Territory created Phillips County, covering the southeast portion of the territory, and Miller County on the Red River.[8]

Four of the new counties, Lawrence, Clark, Hempstead, and Miller, were in areas not mentioned by the census of 1810 and far removed from those that were. In the census of 1820, these counties were home to 69 percent of the 14,273 people then living in Arkansas. Lawrence County alone had 5,602 persons; Clark County had 1,040; Hempstead County was home to 2,248; and 999 people lived on the west side of Red River in Miller County. Arkansas County, Phillips County, and Pulaski County, which included eastern Arkansas and the Arkansas River, the earlier centers of population, contained only 4,384 persons, 31 percent of the whole.[9] (See figure 2.)

Arkansas became a separate territory after Missouri applied for statehood and asked for a southern boundary at 36 degrees 30 minutes—this boundary was later dropped to 36 degees east of the St. Francis River, creating a "bootheel" to accommodate settlers in lower New Madrid County who wished to stay in Missouri. Settlers from Arkansas petitioned for territorial status and were supported by the territorial delegate from Missouri and Rep. George Robertson of Kentucky, who offered a resolution to that effect. For a time, however, Arkansas was embroiled in the issues of the Missouri Compromise as Congress debated the wisdom of allowing slavery in the new territory. After a lively and close fight, the "peculiar institution" was allowed to continue in Arkansas because it was located south of 36 degrees, 30 minutes, the latitude that was emerging as the boundary between future slave and free states created from the Louisiana Purchase. Arkansas Territory was officially born in March of 1819.[10]

As a separate territory, Arkansas began to get more attention and to undergo more change. Within a year its citizens had elected a territorial legislature and a delegate to represent them in Congress. In 1821 the territorial government moved its capital from Arkansas Post to Little Rock, which was closer to the center of the state and the locus of population. In other developments, the United States government made its presence felt by constructing Fort Smith, which was substantially complete in 1820.

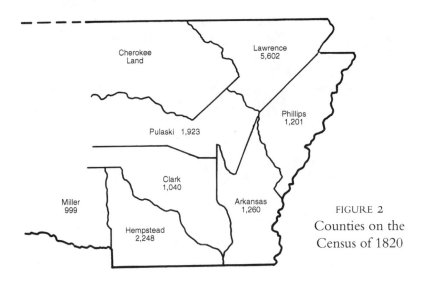

FIGURE 2

Counties on the Census of 1820

Located on the Arkansas River at Belle Point, on the western border of present-day Arkansas, this army post was charged with keeping peace among the Indians of the Southwest. The United States also began to survey public land in 1815 and was offering it for sale by 1822. The territory's first newspaper, the *Arkansas Gazette*, began publishing in 1819. The next year the steamboat *Comet* arrived at Arkansas Post, the first of many such vessels that would ply the Arkansas and White rivers, and later the Red River, linking the new territory with New Orleans and other markets.[11]

Less positive from the standpoint of white settlers in Arkansas was the Indian policy of the United States, which seemed for a time to have designated the new territory as a homeland for Native Americans. In 1818, the Quapaws, who numbered about five hundred persons, had ceded their traditional claims to an enormous body of land located between the Arkansas, Canadian, and Red rivers but kept title to a tract lying along the south side of the Arkansas River between Arkansas Post and Little Rock and extending south to the Ouachita River. The legislature of Arkansas Territory called for the complete ouster of the Quapaws, claiming that the holdings amounted to twenty square miles per tribal member. The *Arkansas Gazette* indicated the seriousness of the problem, pointing out that the Indians were occupying land "toward which many of our citizens, and numerous strangers, many of whom are respectable and wealthy planters from Alabama, Tennessee, &c . . . have for a long time cast a wishful eye." In 1824 Congress provided funds, and Robert Crittenden, acting governor of Arkansas Territory, coerced the Quapaws into selling their remaining land in Arkansas and joining the Caddos on the Louisiana side of the Red River.[12]

Less easy to deal with was the Indian population of northwest Arkansas. In 1808, by the Treaty of Fort Clark, the United States had forced the Osages to give up all claims to land east of a line that ran south from the Missouri River, passing near present-day Springdale, Arkansas, and intersecting the Arkansas River at Frog's Bayou, located a few miles east of present-day Van Buren.[13] The removal of these fierce natives was a boon to white settlement, but it was offset immediately by the arrival of substantial numbers of Cherokees from east of the Mississippi. A few Cherokees had moved into Arkansas in the 1790s to escape from conflicts with the Americans. Anxious to remove the rest of the nation, President Thomas Jefferson, early in 1809, offered the Cherokee chiefs land between the Arkansas and White rivers where the Osages used to hunt. The Cherokees were to get as many acres in Arkansas as they would give up in the east. In 1817, the United States put this principle into a treaty that defined the new Cherokee territory as lying west of a diagonal line running from Shield's Ferry on the White River near modern Batesville to Point Remove on the Arkansas River near present-day Morrillton.[14]

By the early 1820s, there were some three thousand Cherokee Indians living in Arkansas, most of them along the Arkansas River between Point Remove and Mulberry Creek. Conflict between the Cherokees and the Osages to the west led Cherokee agent William Lovely to negotiate an agreement with the Osages by which they sold back to the United States a large tract of land between the 1808 boundary and the Verdigris River in what is now Oklahoma. Lovely's Purchase, as the tract was known, came into existence in 1818. It was designed to be a buffer zone where the Cherokees could hunt without getting into fights with the Osages, but instead it became a source of contention between the Cherokees and the citizens of Arkansas Territory. President James Monroe had told the Cherokees that they would always have an outlet to the west, and they believed Lovely's Purchase was their land, although in fact it belonged to the United States.[15]

The attitude of white settlers in Arkansas toward the Cherokees is illustrated by a letter published in the *Arkansas Gazette* that accused the treaty of 1817 of "turning loose a ferocious band of blood-thirsty marauding savages . . . on a defenseless people."[16] In 1823 the Arkansas legislature complained about the "numerous hoards of Savages who have heretofore existed and who Still are Crowding in upon our frontier" and asked the United States for more military protection against both the Osages and the Cherokees.[17] Aware that Lovely's Purchase included some of the finest land in the territory, the whites wanted to be able to settle there. Not until 1828 was the issue finally settled when the Cherokees were removed west of a line running from the southwestern corner of Missouri to the Arkansas River near Fort Smith, which became the northern portion of Arkansas's western boundary.[18] (See figure 3.)

Despite the fact that few of them ever moved to Arkansas, it was the Choctaws who caused the most consternation among the early citizens of Arkansas Territory. In 1820 Andrew Jackson negotiated the Treaty of Doaks Stand by which the Choctaw Nation agreed to give up about a third of its land in southwestern Mississippi for a new home in Arkansas. The Arkansas land had been selected by Secretary of War John C. Calhoun, who knew about the Quapaw cession but had little other information about the territory. Beginning at Point Remove on the Arkansas River across from the terminus of the Cherokee boundary line, the Choctaw Line, as it was called, ran southwest to the Red River at the mouth of Little River near present-day Foreman, Arkansas. West of that boundary the

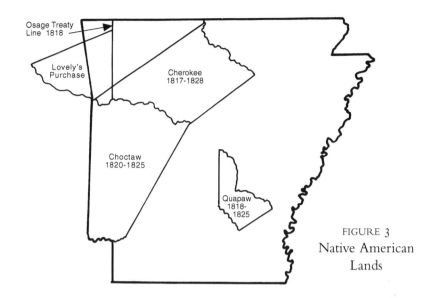

Osage Treaty Line 1818

Lovely's Purchase

Cherokee 1817-1828

Choctaw 1820-1825

Quapaw 1818-1825

FIGURE 3
Native American
Lands

Choctaws gained title to some thirteen million acres between the Arkansas and Canadian rivers on the north and the Red River on the south.[19]

Unknown to Calhoun and Jackson, they had also given the Choctaws a significant part of Arkansas Territory. Based on the census of 1820, the Choctaw Line cut off all of Miller County and large parts of Hempstead, Clark, and Pulaski counties; in that area, the rich farmland visited by William Stevenson, lived a quarter to a third of the territorial population.

William Woodruff, editor of the *Arkansas Gazette*, voiced an outrage that was general. He denounced the Choctaw Treaty, claiming that "our country is now nearly over-run by marauding savages." Equally compelling and more accurate was his assertion that the Choctaw lands would include parts of four and perhaps five Arkansas counties and in them "several respectable and flourishing settlements." Woodruff referred to the Choctaws as "poor deluded wretches" and, somewhat inconsistently, claimed that their presence exposed the white population to "the aggressions of a fierce and savage enemy." Finally, the feisty editor asserted that if the federal government intended Arkansas to become a "Botany Bay" for the Indians, it should disband the territorial government and cease to encourage the immigration of whites.[20]

James Woodson Bates, the Arkansas delegate to Congress, complained loudly about the treaty and found support among western legislators. In the spring of 1821, the *Arkansas Gazette* reported that President Monroe had assured Congress that a new treaty would be made with the Choctaws and that in the meantime any Indians removed to Arkansas would "be sent far west as not to interfere with the white settlements." When nothing had happened a year later, however, Woodruff was discouraged and began to believe that sectional politics was behind the inactivity: northern states were trying to slow Arkansas's movement toward statehood and advance that of Michigan. Perhaps Arkansas was to be subjected to "an 'Egyptian pilgrimage' under a Territorial government." Meanwhile, the Choctaws stayed in Mississippi, and the settlers of southwestern Arkansas continued to occupy the land they were on. Finally, in 1825 a new treaty was negotiated and a revised boundary was surveyed south from Fort Smith to the Red River. Arkansas did lose most of Miller County as well as part of Crawford County to the north. The *Arkansas Gazette* estimated that three thousand citizens were dispossessed by the revised Choctaw Line, which, nonetheless, became the southern portion of Arkansas's western boundary.[21]

While its Indian affairs were being settled, Arkansas Territory continued to grow. During the 1820s the population increased at a less rapid rate than in the previous decade, in part because the Panic of 1819 and the ensuing depression slowed the westward migration of the American people. The 14,273 Arkansans of 1820 grew to 30,388 in 1830, increasing at a rate of 8 percent per year, slightly higher than that of Missouri. During the same period the number of counties in the territory rose from seven to twenty-three. Northwest Arkansas was an important area of growth beginning in 1827 when the territorial legislature created Lovely County west of the upper Cherokee boundary and the Osage line of 1808. Much larger than Lovely's Purchase, Lovely County included more of present-day Oklahoma than of present-day Arkansas. The Oklahoma portion was lost to Arkansas in 1828 by the Cherokee Treaty of that year, and most of what was left became Washington County in 1828. Two years later Washington County had more than 2,000 people.[22]

American expansion to the west picked up steam in the 1830s. Between 1830 and 1840, the population of Arkansas rose from 30,388 to 97,574, growing at an annual rate of 12 percent. The settlers of Arkansas were from the South for the most part. Tennessee was a particularly important source of immigration, behind it was Missouri, with Mississippi and Alabama also significant. In 1840, four years after statehood, Arkansas still exhibited a frontier demography. There were fewer than two inhabitants for each square mile of land. In the white population that numbered 77,174 persons, men were more numerous than women by a ratio of three to two. The settlers were also youthful compared with other white Americans. Children under ten were 32 percent of the American population, but 38 percent of the population in Arkansas; adults over sixty were 4 percent of the American population as a whole, but only 2 percent of the population in Arkansas. Young families and single men were attracted to the frontier in the nineteenth century, and Arkansas Territory was no exception.[23]

The demographic peculiarities of the white settlers were not echoed in the slave population, which numbered 19,935 persons in 1840 and was 20 percent of the American population. There were only 107 men for each 100 women among slaves between twenty-four and thirty-five years old, apparently because few planters brought single males or groups of males when they migrated. Most of the slaves in Arkansas were located in the southern and eastern portion of the state, creating a pattern that would match that of cotton production and plantation agriculture.[24]

Despite its growth in population, Arkansas lagged behind its peers. Missouri, not too much older than Arkansas, had nearly four times as many people, and Michigan, which became a state in 1837, had more than twice as many. Part of the problem was the Indian removal policy of the United States, which caused uncertainty among settlers and would-be settlers and circumscribed their economic opportunities. It has also been suggested that the Indian Territory slowed the development of Arkansas by blocking the movement of settlers going west. In this view Arkansas was a population mill pond, out of the mainstream as the westward migration flowed through Missouri and Louisiana. Another obstacle was the rugged terrain of the Arkansas highlands: large areas in both the Ouachita and Ozark mountains were ill suited to farming and were settled only slowly and sparsely.[25]

Transportation was also a problem. The swamp that extended along the line of the St. Francis River in eastern Arkansas posed a formidable barrier to overland travel, and it was a long time before the territory had usable roads. Steamboat transportation was impossible in periods of low water and dangerous in the best of times, but more than eighty of the mechanical vessels operated in Arkansas Territory. When Capt. Henry Shreve cleared the Red River Raft—a tangled mass of fallen trees and vegetation that obstructed the river for more than a hundred miles below modern Shreveport—in the mid-1830s the possibility of steam navigation on that river caused a land boom in southwestern Arkansas.[26] The unflattering reputation that Arkansas Territory developed very early may also have discouraged immigrants. The *Arkansas Advocate*, Little Rock's second newspaper, reported in 1830 that people in Memphis were attempting to keep settlers there by attacking Arkansas with "the most vile and false slanders respecting the roads, the soil, the morals of the inhabitants" and the climate. Arkansans were described as "destitute of moral honesty

[and] reckless of human life."[27] True or not, these criticisms were part of a larger pattern of negative descriptions.

~

The lives of Arkansans, counted and catalogued by the United States Census, were also observed and described by travelers to Arkansas in a manner much more haphazard and subjective but also richer in detail. These accounts, some of which were published, created the Bear State image of Arkansas, a stereotype that emphasized the wild nature of the place and the fondness of its inhabitants for hunting. According to these accounts, the settlers of the Bear State were occasionally charming, but more often they were violent and lawless. Enthusiastic for the hunt, they showed little other signs of ambition or industry.[28] Were this an accurate analysis, we should expect to find little economic development in Arkansas. Like all stereotypes, however, the Bear State image was based on partial truths that were taken as whole because people wanted to believe them.

The writings of Henry Schoolcraft, the geologist, explorer, and student of American Indians, created a stereotype of the early Arkansan as a hunter who lived for the chase, cherished his dogs above all else, and farmed only as necessary for subsistence. In 1818, the twenty-five-year-old Schoolcraft tramped through the Ozarks while looking for lead deposits.[29] He and a companion left Potosi, Missouri, and walked westerly through an unin-habited region until eventually they made their way down the North Fork of the White River, through what is now Baxter County, Arkansas, and reached the White River itself. Near the mouth of the North Fork, they came to the home of a man named Wells who "had several acres of ground in a state of cultivation, and a substantial new-built log-house, consisting of one room."

Schoolcraft was impressed with the evidence of a hunting lifestyle: animal skins were curing on the side of the cabin; the children wore "abundantly dirty and greasy" buckskin clothing; guns, antlers, deerskin bags of bear oil and honey hung from the walls, and homemade furniture filled the Wells' home. Wells and his wife also talked about hunting most of the time, although she also fed the travelers a meal that consisted mostly of domesticated food: "smoking-hot corn bread, butter, honey, and milk, a diet we should at anytime have relished. "[30]

Leaving the Wells' home, Schoolcraft and his companion traveled up the White River into a still more remote area. They spent time with at least one other family and eventually reached a place called Sugar-Loaf Prairie where four more families were located. Schoolcraft was now moved to generalize: "In manners, morals, customs, dress, contempt of labor and hospitality, the state of society is not essentially different from that which exists among the savages. Schools, religion, and learning, are alike unknown. Hunting is the principal, the most honourable, and the most profitable employment." Later he would also write about the "hardy, frank, and independent hunters" who had given him "the most hospitable and generous treatment."[31]

The two travelers floated down the White River and picked up the Southwest Trail at Poke Bayou. Thirty miles before reaching that point, Schoolcraft noted that the "bottom lands, as you descend increase in width; the bluffs become more remote." In this area, more congenial to agriculture, the settlers became more numerous. At Poke Bayou there were at least twelve houses and one merchant at a location "advantageous as a commercial and agricultural depot." Leaving the town and heading toward what he called the "Arkansas road," Schoolcraft found "several farms and plantations" and claimed that "the country wears a look of agriculture, industry and increasing population."[32]

Despite this evidence of economic development, Schoolcraft did not revise his view that hunters were the typical settlers of Lawrence County. The weakness of his generalizations as applied to the county as a whole is illustrated by his comments on the mortality of children. He visited one family on the upper White River in which the woman had lost four children before they reached the age of two. Based at least partly on this evidence, Schoolcraft wrote that "the women are observed to have few children" and then explained this phenomenon in terms of the hunter lifestyle and its alleged similarity to "savage life." Whether or not the observation and analysis is correct for hunters, it is manifestly false for the people of Lawrence County, where all of Schoolcraft's observations were made. According to the census of 1820, there were 2.4 children under the age of 10 in Lawrence County for each woman of child-bearing age, while in the United States as a whole there were only 1.7.[33]

Schoolcraft's attitude toward the hunters of Arkansas was influenced by an ethnocentric prejudice in favor of the culture of upstate New York where he was raised. Historian Richard G. Bremer refers to Schoolcraft's "somewhat priggish village-bourgeois outlook," which included a "marked tendency to equate education with respectability." It was this attitude that made him view the hunting lifestyle as a form of savagism, a judgment he would also apply to Indian culture even though he collected Indian myths and married a half-Indian woman.[34] More important here than his negative view of hunters is Schoolcraft's lack of interest in other people. As

George E. Lankford has recently shown, Schoolcraft systematically did not report on the "farmers, mercantilists, and entrepreneurs" he met in the Poke Bayou area.[35]

In fact, the early settlers were both hunters and farmers. William Stevenson described "settlements of industrious people," farmers that is, but "among them many hunters, for wild game, buffalo, bear, deer, beaver, etc., were common." He noted that the farmers also hunted: in 1815, when "the drought had ruined their crops[,] . . . some of them went far up the rivers into the prairies and returned with meat." Sixty years after the event, John Billingsly remembered arriving in 1816 at the Big Mulberry River in western Arkansas where his family lived for two years, mostly on "buffalo, bear, deer, and elk and fish and honey," although they also grew corn and Irish potatoes. John C. Benedict recalled families settled on the Arkansas River near the mouth of Cadron Creek in 1818 who were subsisting entirely on wild game, although within a year or so some of them had constructed a water-driven grist mill.[36] Subsistence hunting seems to have been a temporary phenomenon for most settlers, soon replaced by agriculture. David Musick and William Parker, who visited southwest Arkansas for Governor Clark in 1816, found "the improvements[—]fine farms [with] elegantly Cultivated fields[,] luxuriant Crops of Corn and numerous heads of cattle[,] horses[, and] hogs &c[—]that are to be met with in this quarter are strong proofs of the exertions & persevering industry of the inhabitants."[37]

More evidence about the early development of agriculture in Arkansas comes from Thomas Nuttall, an English-born botanist, who was ascending the Arkansas River in January of 1819 while Henry Schoolcraft was hiking away from the White River on his way home to Missouri. Only thirty-two years old, Nuttall had already published *Genera of North American Plants with a Catalogue of the Species through 1817*, which won him an international reputation. Funded by friends in the American Philosophical Society and the American Academy of Natural Sciences, the inquisitive and adventurous Nuttall was now on a solitary expedition into Arkansas and what is now Oklahoma in pursuit of more information about American greenery.[38]

Nuttall found a good deal of farming in the lower Arkansas River valley. Cotton was being raised along the river between Arkansas Post and the future site of Little Rock, and the botanist found its "quality no way inferior to that of Red river," presumably in Louisiana. At one settlement, located on "a body of very superior land," the yield was between one thousand and fifteen hundred pounds per acre. Corn also grew very well, with the richest land producing sixty to eighty bushels per acre. There were several cotton gins in the Arkansas Post area and a sawmill near Cadron; a year later on his return from the West, Nuttall found that a grist mill had been built by Wright Daniel just below Little Rock. All in all, it seemed to him "the privations of an infant settlement are beginning to disappear."[39]

Nuttall praised Arkansas for its economic potential: "The territory watered by the Arkansa [sic] is scarcely less fertile than Kentucky[,] . . . the climate is no less healthy, and at the same time favourable to productions more valuable and saleable." But he also found that the settlers of the territory were not making the most of what they had. At Arkansas Post, he lamented that "little attention beyond that of absolute necessity . . . [has] yet been paid to any branch of agriculture." Beef and pork were produced locally, but "potatoes, onions, apples, flour, spirits, wine, and almost every other necessary article of diet, were imported at an enormous price." Cattle were numerous but given neither shelter nor hay, perhaps the reason Nuttall was rarely able to find milk to drink. As he headed west toward Oklahoma, the botanist's judgment was that "the sume of industry calculated to afford any satisfactory experiment in agriculture or domestic economy, has not been exercised by the settlers of Arkansas."[40]

For a glimpse at later developments, we may follow Joseph Meetch, who rode down the Southwest Trail in 1826 and 1827, tracing roughly the route that William Stevenson had taken more than a decade earlier. Between the Missouri border and the White River, Meetch found conditions that were similar to those described by Schoolcraft. He passed a great deal of "second and third rate land" and a number of "poor looking cabins." At a place called De Marrs Mills, near modern Pocahontas, he listened to two locals discuss "the pleasures and advantages accruing from a hunter's life," and he became accustomed to seeing homes that "had a number of Bearskins stretched out to dry."

Once he reached the White River, Meetch found better land and more evidence of civilization. John Magness, who lived near the Little Red River, surprised Meetch with his "good sense and information" and "good language . . . clear of those vulgar and disgusting phrases universally made use of by the middle and lower Classes of the Western people." Magness "was furnishing a small but a tolerable good building with a Stone Chimney two Galeries in front and window," noted Meetch, who contrasted that with the usual structures that had chimneys constructed from "a frame of Short Sticks and daubed over with morter" and windows that are only "holes cut through the logs of the house." Two days later, Meetch reached Little Rock, "handsomely situated on the South bank of the Arkansas, . . . it has a small frame court house and a Jail, three stores and a printing office and contains about 35 houses."

The most negative aspect of Joseph Meetch's account of traveling in Arkansas was his concern for personal safety. Because of "the many murders, robberies, and theft that has been committed," travelers normally banded together, camping out to avoid houses, and "every man has his rifle, tomahawk, butcher knife and very often a dirk and brace of pistols." Meetch worried about himself because he was alone and he did lodge in houses along the way. He carried a knife and two "large pistols" and kept a hand on one of them during an encounter (that ended without trouble) with a pair of strangers on the road south of Little Rock.

While Meetch found Arkansas underdeveloped and lawless, he also became aware of its agricultural potential. Near the Arkansas River he heard Lovely's Purchase widely discussed as "the garden of the Territory." On the banks of the Little Missouri River in the southwest, he found several men building a flatboat sixty feet in length that was to carry their cotton to New Orleans. Most important, he spent several weeks at Mound Prairie, a stretch of land some twenty-five miles long and twelve to fifteen miles wide lying along the north bank of the Red River in what is now Little River County.

Meetch claimed that Mound Prairie contained the "most rich and beautiful scenery" he had ever seen and decided that the area was "the Most desirable part of the Arkansas Territory." Cotton was the staple crop, although other commodities, including peaches, grew easily. The settlers were distinguished by their "disinterested friendship and hospitality to Strangers," but Meetch believed they suffered from economic abundance: "The fertility of the Soil, the peculiarity of the Situation of the County and the moderate temperature of the climate afford such facilities in the accumulation of wealth that it has paved the way to habits of dissipation and gambling, to these demoralizing habits the more wealthy part of the Inhabitants are much addicted." Even in this seeming paradise, however, people in what Meetch called "the lower walks of life" made hunting bears their "chief employ and Sole Amusement" and would give up anything else "for the pleasures of the Chase."[41]

In 1834, eight years after Meetch's trip and two years before Arkansas became a state, the English-born geologist George Featherstonhaugh and his son made the same trip from southeastern Missouri across Arkansas to the Red River. Featherstonhaugh's detailed and published account of Arkansas society emphasized what he believed to be its crudeness, lawlessness, and indolence, but it also provided evidence of the territory's agricultural potential. He was very critical of the meals and lodging he was able to procure while traveling down the Southwest Trail, which was then known as the Military Road. Greasy fried pork, cornbread, bad coffee, and an occasional taste of milk were the staples of settler sustenance, as Featherstonhaugh described it, and the travelers found themselves sleeping in crowded, immodest, and sometimes unclean circumstances.[42]

Like Meetch, Featherstonhaugh found Arkansas a dangerous place. He encountered suspicious and threatening fellows along the trail, and he learned of a man named Childers who had been murdered near the White River. Particularly shocking to Featherstonhaugh's sensibilities was the fact that local vigilantes had attempted to find the killer, but no one had bothered to bury Childers' body, which was allowed to rot in the woods. At Little Rock, Featherstonhaugh found that most of the inhabitants carried pistols or Bowie knives, which he said were originally made for hunting purposes but were now used "for the purpose of slashing and sticking human beings." Traveling down the Arkansas River on a steamboat at the end of his visit, he encountered ten men described as "notorious swindlers and gamblers, who whilst in Arkansas lived by the most desperate cheating and bullying." Boarding at Arkansas Post, these men made their fellow passengers uncomfortable by drinking, cursing, gambling, and brandishing weapons. One "sickly old man" complained about the intense smoke generated by these bullies and was told by one: "If any man tells me he don't like my smoking, I'll put a knife in him." Featherstonhaugh was particularly irked by the fact that the rowdies were joined by two U.S. Army officers and also by Elias Rector, the U.S. marshal of the territory, whom our traveler described as "a man of mean stature, low and sottish in his manners, and as corrupt and reckless as it was possible for [a] human being to be."[43]

Situated in the midst of so much critical comment on Arkansas society, Featherstonhaugh's evidence of economic development is rarely noted. Nonetheless, while writing about southwest Arkansas, in the vicinity of what he called "the little insignificant wooden village of Washington," he praised "the fertility of the soils" that made them "eminently fitted for cotton." "The staple is fine," he noted, adding that it produced fifteen hundred to two thousand pounds in the seed per acre.[44] On his steamboat trip down the Arkansas, Featherstonhaugh saw more cotton plantations. The steamer stopped again and again to load bales, requiring seven hours at one landing and all day at Arkansas Post, where it was impossible to get all of merchant Frederick Notrebe's cotton on board. As it was, the vessel was piled so high that "she looked from the shore like an immense collection of bales of cotton, amongst which some pieces of machinery had been stuck."[45]

A final contributor to the Bear State image was Friedrich Gerstäcker, a traveler from Germany who arrived in Arkansas early in 1838, when he was only twenty years old, and spent lengthy periods in the state over the next three years. Gerstäcker sent long letters home to his mother, which she had published, and which now form a valuable source on life in early Arkansas. In later years, Gerstäcker used the same experiences as the raw materials for the short stories and novels that made him a literary success.[46]

Gerstäcker was a passionate hunter and to him, fresh from Germany, Arkansas was vast and wild, and its most significant inhabitants were the bear, deer, turkeys, and other species of game animals and birds. Which is not to say that he ignored the people; on the contrary, Gerstäcker was more observant and less condescending than most travelers, and he had an instinctive sympathy for the common people of the frontier. He worked on at least two farms, one near the L'Anguille River in eastern Arkansas and the other near the Fourche LaFave River in the central part of the state, and he provides valuable information about farming and rural life. Oil Trove Bottom, for example, the southern bank of the White River below Batesville, Gerstäcker believed was as good as any land in the United States, producing "sixty to seventy bushels of maize to the acre, and pumpkins larger than a man can lift." Describing the circumstances of his friend Hilger, who lived along the Little Red River, Gerstäcker sketched what most Arkansas settlers probably considered the good life: "He had bought the land, had a pair of horses, several head of cattle and pigs, and lived happy and independent in the circle of his family." But hunting and hunters loom large in Gerstäcker's letters, and animals drop with a frequency that would make a modern sportsman envious. On the other hand, he says little about plantation agriculture or state politics and writes about Little Rock only briefly and negatively. Small wonder that a modern editor of his narrative states that "Arkansas was all but completely wild."[47]

Insight into the nature of Arkansas's Bear State image comes from Grady McWhiney's recent study of cracker culture, a pattern of behavior that McWhiney associates with southern whites of the antebellum period. McWhiney and Forrest McDonald believe that this culture is derived from the Celtic heritage of the South, which they trace to the eighteenth-century immigration of Scots-Irish and other peoples from Ireland and the upland areas of England, Wales, and Scotland. The South, says McWhiney, was "ideally suited for the clannish, herding, leisure-loving Celts, who relished whiskey, gambling, and combat, and who despised hard work, anything English, most government, fences and any other restraints on them or their free-ranging livestock."[48] Documenting the existence of Celtic influences in southern society, McWhiney cites an impressive array of antebellum commentators complaining about the laziness of southerners, the slovenly agricultural practices they followed, the poor food and accommodations they provided, and their excessive attention to pleasure, propensity for violence, and indifference to progress. Many of these comments were made by northerners, who took, in McWhiney's view, the same superior and critical perspective on the agricultural South that the lowland English had taken toward the underdeveloped society of their Celtic neighbors.[49]

Whether it is Celtic or not, the culture described by McWhiney is clearly southern, and just as surely it is the culture that created the Bear State image of Arkansas. Cracker culture first shows up in the eighteenth-century backcounty, and it remains highly visible in the western movement of the South that carried people into Arkansas.[50] As the most rugged and remote frontier of the South, Arkansas seems to have exhibited cracker culture in an extreme form that caught the attention of visitors. Indeed, unadulterated versions of it persisted in remote areas of the Arkansas highlands for a long time. Building a textile mill on the Little Missouri River in the Ouachita Mountains in 1860, Henry Merrell found people living in crude log cabins and going barefoot. A Yankee from upstate New York, Merrell had lived in Georgia for seventeen years, yet he was still taken aback by these "mountaineers of Arkansas."[51] His reaction, as we have seen, was hardly novel.

～

The American settlement of Arkansas was an indisputable fact by 1840, its outlines delineated by the census at ten-year intervals, its features sketched by a succession of travelers, and its development given a seal of approval by statehood. After several centuries with little human occupation, the land now held about as many people as it had when de Soto and his Spaniards crossed the Mississippi in 1541. Those people had acquired an image that was both real and mythic. The Bear State concept was real in the sense that crudeness, violence, and a penchant for hunting were very much a part of life in Arkansas, real also in that it reflected the settlement of Arkansas by southern people, many of whom lived in a manner that was looked down upon by northern visitors. The image was mythic, however, because it defined Arkansas society by some characteristics and ignored others, among them the growth of agriculture. Reading travelers' accounts, one might wonder if these modern Arkansans were as materially successful as those who lived three hundred years earlier. Would a modern army have found as much food as did de Soto's troops? In fact, Arkansans were producing an abundance of food by 1840, as we will now attempt to demonstrate.

three

Fruits of the Soil

"Our Territory is rapidly emerging from the sable gloom which so long shrouded and concealed its merits. . . . Its fame spreads as if by the four winds of the earth. . . . Men from every quarter of the Union, and of every profession flock to the fertile and salubrious plains of Arkansas. . . . Large fields of corn, cotton, and tobacco have usurped the dominions of . . . the buffalo and the marauding savage . . . and the earth is made to perform the offices for which she was intended by the God of nature." These lines, attributed to "A Citizen," appeared in the *Arkansas Gazette* in November 1820, a few days before the newspaper moved from Arkansas Post to Little Rock.[1] Rhapsodic though they are, they illustrate both the economic development of Arkansas and the support it received from William Woodruff's newspaper.[2] Agriculture, not hunting or lawlessness, was the preoccupation of the territory, and it became a remarkable success story.

~

A less lyrical and more detailed description of Arkansas Territory and its agricultural potential was published in February of 1823 by Thomas Eskridge, a judge of the Superior Court and a planter in Hempstead County. Eskridge claimed that Arkansas enjoyed "all the advantages of climate, soil, and navigation." The climate was "mild and delightful," and while Arkansas had "the fevers to which all new countries have been found to be subject, . . . they less often terminate fatally than in any country with which we have been acquainted . . . [and] chronic affections are scarcely known."

Eskridge provided a river-by-river description of agricultural potential. The White River was navigable for steamboats and its basin contained much good land, the best of which was "oil trof" bottom, a stretch twenty-five miles by two miles on the south side opposite the mouth of the Black River. The Arkansas River was suitable for steamboats only six months of the year; its bottomlands, however, were "very extensive, in some places 10 to 20 miles wide." Eskridge especially praised Lovely's Purchase, two-and-a-half million acres "of rolling, beautiful country, abounding in fine springs." Located in Crawford County, north of the Arkansas River between Frog Bayou and the Verdigris River, this land was above 35 degrees of latitude, however, making its climate too cold for successful cotton cultivation. The "Great Raft," limited the Red River's use for transportation purposes, but its bottomlands, "frequently three to six miles wide," were more rich than those of the Arkansas. Indeed, wrote Eskridge, land along the Red River was "as rich as human avarice can desire." He lauded Long Prairie and Mount Prairie in particular, although he believed the latter suffered from a lack of water.

Summing up, Judge Eskridge recommended Lawrence County, Independence County, and Crawford County above 35 degrees for wheat, corn, and tobacco. Phillips, Arkansas, Pulaski counties, and the southern part of Crawford County, all of which were on the Mississippi River or the Arkansas River, he found well suited to cotton, corn, and tobacco. Clark, Hempstead, and Miller counties, all on the Red River, were particularly well adapted to cotton cultivation, averaging fifteen hundred pounds to the acre as compared to one thousand in the counties to the north. Eskridge "doubted, indeed, whether any part of the Union be better adapted to cotton, than these counties" on the Red River.

Eskridge made a special pitch to cotton planters who might be considering migrating to Arkansas. He claimed the existing settlers of Arkansas were "people from the slave-holding states, . . . correct in their morals, kind and liberal among one another, and hospitable to strangers." He emphasized "the inducements" that the territory offered to southern planters who could, in his opinion, earn a three hundred dollars profit yearly for each able-bodied hand employed along the Red River, where the slave could cultivate ten acres of cotton and ten acres of corn and pick five acres of the cotton.[3]

There was some basis to Eskridge's optimism. As early as 1822 the *Arkansas Gazette* noted "the general disposition which prevails among our citizens to cultivate . . . large crops of cotton," an attitude strengthened by a New Orleans price of around twenty cents a pound. In April of that year, the newspaper reported that planters in Hempstead County had shipped some four hundred bales of cotton to New Orleans during the previous season and were beginning to focus all their energies on that commodity. By 1825, cotton, for the *Gazette,* had become the "staple production of our Territory." A letter from Arkansas Post in December of that year declared that the town was "in a bustle" as cotton-laden boats arrived at the landing and wagon teams of cotton and cottonseed filled the streets. Frederick Notrebe, the principal merchant, was paying the New Orleans price in cash for local cotton and storing it in anticipation of a rising market. The newness of cotton production in Arkansas County was underlined by the writer, who referred to "our planters, who are just now deserving of the name." Cotton was also being produced in less likely areas. Crawford County, located north of the Arkansas River in western Arkansas, was expected to produce two hundred bales, and Batesville, in Independence County, anticipated the export of four hundred bales. Woodruff exulted in the growing "reputation of Arkansas, as an excellent cotton-growing country."[4]

Corn was a much less heralded but vigorous number-two crop. Consumed at home both by humans and livestock, corn was also sold, sometimes in New Orleans, but more often to immigrant settlers or to the federal government, which supplied it to troops and to the Indians under its control. Corn was grown in place of cotton when the market for "the staple crop" was particularly low. During the decade of the 1820s, corn in the ear sold for about fifty cents a bushel in Arkansas. In the summer of 1822, Isaac Watkins opened a "Horse Mill" in Little Rock that would grind six bushels of corn in an hour, and more "by a little pushing of the horses." The charge was one-fourth of the meal if the mill horses were used, one-eighth if the customer employed his own animals.[5] Most of the cornmeal consumed in the territory, nonetheless, was ground at home.

Arkansans also began to produce vegetables and fruits, and they seem to have become largely self-sufficient in those commodities. The *Arkansas Gazette* was ever solicitous about the effects of weather on "gardens" and "fruit trees," peaches and plums in particular.[6] The only significant agricultural scarcity was wheat, and flour was imported regularly, often from Cincinnati. In 1831, however, Woodruff was pleased to learn that Washington County was producing a "very fine" crop of wheat. He looked forward to the day when local wheat would supply the demand of the territory and "thus circulate among our own farmers the thousands of dollars which annually go up the Ohio for that article."[7]

Arkansas Territory developed an agricultural economy during the decade of the 1820s, if we may believe an essayist in the *Gazette* who called himself "Franklin." In a piece titled "Our Territory," which appeared in January of 1831, he declared that Arkansas "was a wilderness" in 1819 and that "large and well cultivated farms are now to be found in almost every part of the Territory." Taking pleasure in the increased population of Arkansas reported by the census of 1830, this writer believed that the territory would shortly become a state. Franklin stated that "the great mass" of Arkansans were "enterprising and industrious citizens distinguished for integrity in the private transactions, and for love of liberty and love of order." There were also, he allowed, tempering his boosterism with realism, "some individuals of depraved minds and bad habits."[8] None of this, of course, applied to the slaves, whose labor Franklin and his readers took for granted.

～

The *Arkansas Gazette* is a useful but limited source for studying the development of the Arkansas economy. Editor Woodruff supported Arkansas agriculture, but usually in an anecdotal fashion based on scraps of information that came into his hands and on the topics that interested his correspondents or were solicited from them. The coverage was neither systematic—it emphasized cotton—nor well documented, particularly with respect to the size of production for the various commodities. Fortunately there are two large data bases that allow for a more comprehensive and detailed analysis, particularly in the decade of the 1830s. One of these data bases is the tax records for the period and the other is the census of 1840. Each of them requires some explanation.

Arkansas Territory taxed its citizens separately for the support of territorial and county governments, and the state of Arkansas continued the practice. An assessment of property for both purposes was carried out at the county level by the sheriff, who was also responsible for collecting the taxes. Taxes were assessed on a variety of different kinds of property, including billiard tables and "carriages of pleasure," but this study focuses on slaves, land, cattle, and horses, which formed the great bulk of taxable property. A poll tax that applied to free white males over the age of 21 insured that their names would be on the assessment roles whether or not they owned taxable property.[9] County tax assessments are extant for a few counties on a scattered basis in the 1820s and become more numerous by the mid-1830s. The data base used here consists of a random sample of 987 taxpayers drawn from the 10,000 or so names on the 25 county tax assessments that are extant for the 39 counties in 1840.[10]

The census of 1840 was the first national census to collect detailed information about agriculture, providing county totals for crop production and livestock ownership. One must, however, approach this data with some caution. Inaccuracies in this census, apparently produced by the complex forms used by the enumerators, created a sectional controversy by seeming to show that insanity was more prevalent among northern blacks than those in the South. Moreover, in 1900, Carroll Wright, the respected commissioner of Labor, declared that all attempts "to include statistics of industry" in censuses down through 1840 "were of little avail . . . and the results . . . have but little value."[11] Wright's judgment was too harsh and too sweeping, however. Agricultural totals from the 1840 census are included, for example, in the highly respected tables of *Historical Statistics of the United States.*[12] As we shall see, the Arkansas figures from 1840 are roughly congruent with data from the tax records of Arkansas, and they also fit well with those from later, more reliable, censuses.

Agricultural activity in Arkansas was conditioned by the geographical division of the area into lowland and highland regions. The lowlands include the Mississippi Delta, an alluvial plain in the eastern portion of the state, and a coastal plain in the south. Along a line running diagonally from southwest to northeast, the lowlands give way to highlands, the Ouachita Mountains to the west and the Ozark Mountains to the north. The lowland and highland regions divide Arkansas rather evenly, and each contained about half of the population. The lowland region, with its milder climate, flat terrain, and deep, rich soil was better suited to the production of cotton and thus was more attractive to slaveholders. By 1840 slaves made up 31 percent of the population in the lowlands and only 10 percent in the highlands. (See figure 4.) By good fortune, the existing tax records for 1840 were distributed around the state so that 40 percent of the sample taxpayers came from the lowland region that included 43 percent of the white population.[13] With respect to the lowland and highland regions, the sample may be considered unbiased.

Both the census of 1840 and the tax records for that year list slaves, horses, and cattle. The tax assessment, however, counted only those slaves over eight years old and under sixty years old and horses and cattle over three years old. Table 1 provides the number of each type of property for each data base calculated on the basis of one hundred inhabitants. The tax records show far fewer slaves, horses, and cattle than the census, as one would expect, but the difference is not simply a matter of the tax assessment applying to a smaller population. Slaves over eight and under sixty were about 68 percent of the slave population. The eleven taxable slaves per one hundred inhabitants thus represent sixteen slaves of all ages, but this is still 20 percent fewer than those counted by the census. The gap between the

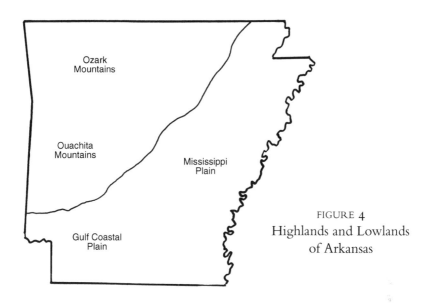

Ozark
Mountains

Ouachita
Mountains

Mississippi
Plain

Gulf Coastal
Plain

FIGURE 4
Highlands and Lowlands
of Arkansas

two enumerations is a significant one; on the other hand, it is not difficult to believe that slave owners found ways to minimize the number of their taxable slaves when the assessor was doing his work. It is impossible to know what percentage of horses and cattle would have been older than three years, although the shorter natural life span of cattle and the fact that many would have been slaughtered for food makes it clear why the taxable cattle were so much less a percentage of the census cattle than were the taxable horses.

TABLE I
Slaves, Horses, and Cattle in 1840
Per 100 Persons, U.S. Census and County Tax Records

	Census	*Tax Records*	*Percent on Tax Records*
Slaves	20 (all)	11 (9–59 years)	55
Horses	53 (all)	28 (over 3 years)	53
Cattle	193 (all)	69 (over 3 years)	36

A more convincing argument for consistency between the census and the tax records is the strikingly similar way they divide slaves, horses, and cattle between the highland region and the lowland region. Table 2 gives the number of each type of property per one hundred inhabitants by region for both data sets and also the ratio of the highland amount to the lowland amount. While census takers and tax assessors came up with different numbers, the distribution between the two regions is almost exactly the same for all three categories of property. Thus it seems reasonable to proceed with an analysis of the Arkansas economy, recognizing that the data is not perfect, but also that it is not terribly flawed either.

TABLE 2
Slaves, Horses, and Cattle in 1840 Per 100 Persons
U.S. Census and County Tax Records, Highlands and Lowlands

	Census			Tax Records		
	Highlands	*Lowlands*	*Ratio*	*Highlands*	*Lowlands*	*Ratio*
Slaves	10	31	.31	6	17	.35
Horses	62	43	1.44	31	24	1.29
Cattle	184	203	.91	66	73	.90

Note: Ratio = Highlands/Lowlands

The census of 1840 indicates the success of Arkansas agriculture, but only if one computes per capita figures rather than comparing total production. Missouri, for example, produced over seventeen million bushels of corn, dwarfing the five million produced in Arkansas; but Arkansas had only a quarter as many people as did Missouri, and Arkansans actually grew more corn per person than did Missourians. Total production numbers are important in ranking the states, but relating production to people is a much more useful way of understanding both productivity and economic welfare. Table 3 compares Arkansas with its neighboring states with respect to the ownership of livestock and the production of crops per one hundred persons.

TABLE 3
Livestock and Produce, Arkansas and Neighboring States in 1840
Per 100 Persons

	Ark.	*Mo.*	*Tenn.*	*Miss.*	*La.*
LIVESTOCK					
Horses	53	51	41	29	28
Cattle	193	113	99	166	101
Swine	403	331	353	267	86

TABLE 3   CONTINUED

	Ark.	*Mo.*	*Tenn.*	*Miss.*	*La.*
MAJOR ARKANSAS CROPS					
Cotton, lbs.	6,179	32	3,341	51,437	43,340
Corn, bush	4,967	4,517	5,425	3,504	1,585
MINOR ARKANSAS CROPS					
Tobacco, lbs.	152	2,363	3,564	22	22
Wheat, bush	109	357	551	52	0
Oats, bush	194	583	848	178	29
Potatoes, bush	301	204	23	434	222

For the size of its population, cotton production in Arkansas was very small compared to cotton production in Mississippi and Louisiana, but it was twice that of Tennessee. Corn production in Arkansas was slightly behind that of Tennessee but above all other neighboring states. Arkansas produced more wheat and oats than Mississippi and Louisiana but less than Tennessee and Missouri. Arkansas grew little tobacco, which was an important crop in Tennessee and Missouri. In livestock production, Arkansas was the clear regional leader. There was a horse for every two persons in the state, nearly two head of cattle for each human being, and hogs outnumbered people four to one. Missouri had as many horses, Mississippi was close in cattle, and Missouri and Tennessee were not far behind in hogs. The value of poultry was estimated by census takers, and Arkansas led with a valuation of $1.12 per person, followed by Mississippi at 98 cents, and the other states at about 75 cents.[14]

Cotton, "the staple production" of Arkansas according to the *Arkansas Gazette,* was produced on a regional basis. Ninety-one percent of it was grown in ten counties, nine of which were located in the lowlands. Only Johnson County on the upper Arkansas River was a major cotton producer among highland counties. The remaining nine counties were located in the southern portion of the lowlands, and all were drained by navigable rivers: Chicot and Phillips by the Mississippi, Arkansas and Jefferson by the Arkansas, Union and Clarke by the Ouachita, and Lafayette, Sevier, and Hempstead by the Red. Fifty-eight percent of the slaves in Arkansas lived in these ten counties, and only 24 percent of the white population. Two counties, Chicot in the southeast portion of the state, and Lafayette in the southwest, produced 40 percent of Arkansas's cotton. Twenty-two percent of all Arkansas slaves lived in these two counties and only about two percent of the white population. (See figure 5.)

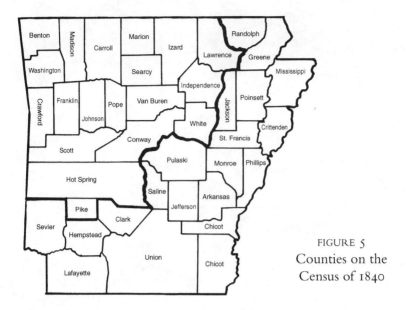

FIGURE 5
Counties on the
Census of 1840

The 1840 cotton crop was marketed in New Orleans for only about 8 cents a pound, significantly lower than the usual 15 cents a pound that had been paid back in 1834 and 1835. Even at 8 cents, however, it was estimated in *Niles Weekly Register* that planters farming the new lands in the Southwest might make a profit of $110 to $140 for each working slave. Thus the gross proceeds of the Arkansas cotton crop, some $482,291, must have brought considerable income to the planters of Chicot, Lafayette, and other lowland counties who used slave labor to produce high yields on their fertile soil.[15]

Corn was much more widely grown in Arkansas than was cotton. Per capita production was 46 bushels in the lowlands and 53 bushels in the highlands. Only 5 of the 39 counties had a per capita production under 40 bushels. While cotton produced individual wealth in an unparalleled manner, corn may have produced more income for the state. During the territorial years there were times when a bushel of corn could be sold for as much as $2.00, but usually the price was much lower. Alfred Dupuy of Lawrence died in 1840 leaving an estate that included 125 bushels of corn valued at 25 cents each.[16] At that modest rate, the Arkansas surplus was worth $480,000 or an average of $39 for each white household.

Corn was a basic element in the diet of Arkansans, and it was also used to fatten livestock. Sam Hilliard has provided a formula for determining the subsistence need for corn in the South based on the assumption that each eating unit, that is one adult or two children under 15 years, required 13 bushels annually, a hog needed 4 bushels, and a horse needed 7.5

bushels.[17] On that basis, the 4.9 million bushels of corn produced in Arkansas would have resulted in a surplus of 1.9 million bushels. If Hilliard's formula is correct, Arkansas farmers could provide for themselves and their livestock and then supply the complete corn needs for a year of another 148,000 adults.

The minor crops of Arkansas agriculture were produced mostly in the highlands, with the exception of potatoes, which were grown widely around the state. Counties along the Missouri border led in wheat production, with Lawrence County and Izard County producing at roughly the per capita rate achieved by Missouri. Overall, the wheat production of the highlands was 1.75 bushels per capita, markedly above the .42 of the lowland but still well below the rate for Missouri and Tennessee. Washington County led Arkansas in growing oats, with 6.62 bushels per capita, a specialization that was probably related to an emphasis there on the breeding of horses. The highlands average was 2.56 bushels compared to 1.32 in the lowlands. Searcy County and its neighbor Izard County led Arkansas in the production of tobacco, yet even in these counties per capita production was dwarfed by that of Missouri and Tennessee.

In his 1948 study, *Plain Folk of the Old South,* Frank Owsley emphasized the importance of livestock in the southern economy, particularly in areas like Arkansas where relatively little land was under cultivation. Owsley claimed that many southerners were full-time herdsmen who raised cattle and hogs on the open range, at first on the grasslands of the frontier and later in hilly and forested areas where they were pushed by the farmers and planters. Travelers thought these backwoods people were lazy and shiftless because they grew few crops and seemed to work very little, but Owsley believed these hasty passers-by overlooked the "herds of cows and droves of hogs" hidden amid the forests and rugged terrain and feeding on the mast and vegetation. More recently, Forrest McDonald and Grady McWhiney have argued that herdsmen were not a frontier or backwoods phenomenon but rather a substantial and permanent element of the economy. In their view, raising livestock on the open range was an expression of the Celtic ethnicity that created what McWhiney calls cracker culture. By contrast, Sam Hilliard recognized the existence of herders, but claimed that most livestock were owned by farmers and planters and that the latter often owned large and diversified herds of cattle that were well cared for by regional standards.[18]

In Arkansas, the livestock industry seems to have been closely tied to agricultural activity in general, as Hilliard has suggested. We can illustrate that point by looking at the size and distribution of cattle herds, an exercise that also provides much insight into the nature of Arkansas farms and plantations. (See Table 4.) It must be remembered, however, that taxable cattle are those over three years old, and they constitute only 36 percent of the cattle enumerated by the census; moreover, the census takers ignored all cattle less than one year old. Thus the average head of taxable cattle represents three to four actual cattle. The median "very small" cattle herd of Table 4 would have six or eight animals, the "small herd" twelve to sixteen, the "large herd" twenty-four to thirty, and the "very large" herd sixty to eighty.

A glance at Table 4 indicates that the ownership of horses, land, and slaves is related to the ownership of cattle in a positive manner. Even though we do not know what crops, if any, were grown by individual taxpayers, larger cattle herds seem to be associated with agricultural success rather than with a separate herding function. Southern herders practiced open range grazing, allowing their animals to forage on the grasslands or the forests of the public domain, or on untilled land even if it were in private hands. Herders sometimes owned land but usually in small amounts. Were most cattle owners herders, we would expect no relationship, or even a negative relationship, between the size of the herds and the amount of land owned.

TABLE 4

Taxable Property and Section by Herds of Taxable Cattle

| | Herds of Taxable Cattle | | | |
	Very Small N=208	Small N=189	Large N=186	Very Large N=75
CATTLE				
mean	1.5	4.0	8.6	26.6
median	2.0	4.0	8.0	20.0
ACRES				
mean	33.6	57.2	138.8	473.0
median	0.0	0.0	40.0	193.0
HORSES				
mean	1.3	2.0	3.3	5.8
median	1.0	2.0	3.0	5.0
SLAVES				
mean	0.3	0.3	1.3	4.4
median	0.0	0.0	0.0	2.0
SECTION				
lowlands	29%	29%	46%	55%
highlands	71%	71%	54%	45%

This would be particularly true in Arkansas in 1840, where there were fewer than two people per square mile and a vast amount of land remained in public hands. In our sample, however, the amount of acreage owned by cattle owners increased regularly with the size of their herds. Most Arkansas cattlemen, it would seem, also cultivated the soil and on a scale commensurate with their animal husbandry. Moreover, the owners of "very large" herds were a well-to-do group by Arkansas standards: their median taxable wealth was in the ninety-first percentile for all sample taxpayers. Larger cattle herds were also more likely than smaller herds to be found in the lowlands. Their location, their land, and their slaves suggests that these owners of "very large" herds were part of an emerging planter class.

On the other hand, there probably were some herders, and perhaps quite a few, who did little or no farming. Even among the owners of "very large" herds, 35 percent did not own slaves and 24 percent did not own land. Among these was the largest cattle owner in the sample, J. W. Lamburston of Independence County, whose herd of 180 taxable cattle was more than twice the size of the next largest herd and probably included more than 600 animals.

Arkansas cattle were numerous and ubiquitous but not extremely valuable. There were nearly two head of cattle for each person in the state, and three quarters of the taxpayers with any taxable wealth at all owned at least one cow. Taxable cattle were assessed at an average of thirteen dollars each, but they constituted only 5 percent of taxable wealth; horses, by contrast, were assessed at an average of sixty-three dollars and made up 9 percent of taxable wealth. The open-range system meant that cattle owners provided their animals with little hay or other domestic forage, gave them no shelter, and paid scant attention to their breeding. As a consequence, the livestock were small in size, and the cows gave little milk. Southerners ate three to five times as much pork as they did beef, and dairy products were in limited supply. Still, cattle played a significant role in subsistence, and they could be sold as well. There was a market for beef in New Orleans, and the *Arkansas Gazette* regularly quoted the current prices. The degree to which herds of Arkansas cattle and swine were driven south or shipped by steamboat to Louisiana is simply not clear. The United States government also bought beef to use as rations for the Indians under its control, and it occasionally purchased cattle to build up Indian herds.[19]

Swine were distributed around Arkansas in a pattern similar to that of corn; they were more prevalent in the highlands than the lowlands but found all over the state. The 4 hog per capita figure for Arkansas was generated by an average of 3.5 in the lowlands and 4.5 in the highlands. Saline

County in the central Arkansas lowlands was the only county in the state with less than 2 hogs per capita.

Hilliard's measure of subsistence in the production of hogs is based on an annual consumption by eating units of 150 pounds of pork, the potential annual butchering of 50 percent of all hogs, and a yield of 140 pounds of pork per hog.[20] Using these estimates, there were 118,000 surplus hogs in Arkansas in 1840, a potential pork production of 11 million pounds beyond subsistence needs, enough to provide a year's supply of pork for 110,000 adults. Inventories of estates for this period value hogs at about $3.50 each.[21] If the surplus hogs were sold at that price, they would have yielded $413,000, or $33 for every Arkansas household. And they might have been. For example, whether reflecting popular taste, racial prejudice, or both, the U.S. government bought pork for the troops at Fort Smith, Fort Gibson, and Fort Towson instead of the beef it used to feed the Indians.[22]

～

A useful perspective on Arkansas agriculture in 1840 is obtained by comparing the census figures for that year with those for 1850 and 1860. Table 5 provides data for slaves, livestock, cotton, and corn. One is struck by the overall pattern, an increase in the number of slaves and the production of cotton matched by a decrease in ownership of livestock and the production of corn. Both changes are remarkably consistent, with the exception of the 1850 figure for horses, for which no explanation is apparent. Arkansas in 1840 was a frontier society where settlers were planting corn between the stumps of recently felled trees, and livestock roamed freely in the woods and on the prairies. By 1860, the land was better cleared, there was a higher percentage of slaves in the population, and production was geared less for subsistence and more for the market. Agricultural development was a long-term process, which began, as we have seen, in the early years of the territory.

TABLE 5

Slaves, Livestock, and Produce, Arkansas, 1840, 1850, 1860, Per 100 Persons

	1840	1850	1860
Slaves	20	22	26
Horses	53	34	45
Cattle	193	139	131
Swine	403	399	269
Cotton, 400 lb. bales	15	31	84
Corn, bush.	4,967	4,237	4,093

Another, in some ways more precise, means of examining the development of Arkansas agriculture over time is to look at the changes that took place in Arkansas County between 1825 and 1840, two years for which tax assessments exist. First, however, it is important to say something about the county itself.

When Arkansas Territory was created in 1819, Arkansas County ran along the Mississippi River from Missouri to Louisiana. By 1825, however, the creation of new counties had reduced it to an irregularly shaped land mass of some 2,500 square miles that straddled the Arkansas River and was more or less centered on the village of Arkansas Post. By 1840, Arkansas County was further whittled down to about 1,500 square miles, most of them north of the Arkansas River. Arkansas Post, still the county seat, was now in the extreme southeast corner of the county. Like the rest of the Delta, Arkansas County was relatively flat and contained rich alluvial soil. Its forests were broken by a number of grassy prairies, the largest of which, Grand Prairie, stretched northwest from Arkansas Post for 100 miles and was 10 miles wide in some places.[23]

The American settlers who came to Arkansas County changed the character of local society. By 1823, French inhabitants were not much more than 14 percent of the county total, and they were mostly clustered in Arkansas Post. The new settlers came from southern states for the most part and many of them brought slaves. The black population of Arkansas County was 15 percent of the whole in 1820, 27 percent in 1830, and 28 percent in 1840. By the last date, Arkansas County was a highly productive part of the emerging plantation economy of lowland Arkansas. Its 1,346 inhabitants, 361 of whom were slaves, grew 269 pounds of cotton per capita, second among the 39 counties of Arkansas in 1840; owned 4.64 head of cattle each, the highest number among the counties in the state; and tied for eighth place in hog ownership.

Arkansas County tax assessments show a remarkable increase in the ownership of taxable property between 1825 and 1840 (Table 6). The fact that only 24 percent of the resident taxpayers in 1825 owned land suggests that the others were tenants or even agricultural laborers. In fact, most of them were squatters on the public domain and others were young men living with their parents or other relatives. Still, it is significant that more than half of the taxpayers did not own taxable horses or cattle and that 31 percent of the taxpayers lacked any taxable property at all. The 216 taxpayers of a much smaller Arkansas County in 1840 were far wealthier than those of 1825. The percentage of taxpayers owning slaves, land, horses, and cattle increased dramatically, and the percentage with some sort of taxable property rose 18 points. These changes added up to a large increase in wealth.

Economic growth in taxable property can be measured in precise terms using the mean assessed valuation for each type of property in 1840 and then applying those figures to property held in 1825. Taxable wealth per taxpayers was $834 in 1825 and $1,920 in 1840, a gain of 130 percent for the 15-year period, which represented an average annual growth rate of 5.7 percent. The impact of the increase must have been felt broadly, since the median level of taxable wealth increased from $114 to $400, a gain of 251 percent.

TABLE 6

Ownership of Taxable Property, Arkansas County, 1825 and 1840

	1825 (N=228)		1840 (N=216)	
	Mean	*% Owners*	*Mean*	*% Owners*
Slaves	.55	12	1.48	26
Acres	88.17	24	183.85	43
Cattle	4.22	55	10.26	71
Horses	1.13	47	2.08	68

If many people benefited from economic growth, however, Frederick Notrebe gained more than anyone else. Already a successful businessman, Notrebe built a cotton gin in the early 1820s and became a leading processor and purchaser of the staple crop. His brick store, warehouse, and elegant home stood in stark contrast to the decayed surroundings in the village of Arkansas Post. In 1825, Notrebe owned 800 acres and 8 taxable slaves; by 1840 he owned 5,400 acres and 43 taxable slaves. The increase in his taxable wealth accounted for 18 percent of the growth for the county as a whole. In 1832, the nephew of Governor John Pope dined with Pope at the table of "the opulent" Notrebe and marveled at "a splendid dinner, set out with almost princely magnificence in silver, china and cut-glass."[24]

Other men did well in less spectacular ways. Harold Stillwell, a scion of Joseph Stillwell who had settled a Spanish Grant in 1798, owned 100 acres of land, 1 slave, 2 horses, and 25 cattle in 1825; by 1840, he was assessed for 1,604 acres of land, 2 slaves, 6 horses, and 75 head of cattle. Stillwell's 75 cattle over three years old probably represented a total herd of about 242 head, evidence of the important role of grazing in Arkansas County. Next to Notrebe, the largest slaveowner in the county in 1840 was Lewis Taylor, who owned 27 taxable slaves, 1,020 acres, 5 horses, and 210 head of taxable cattle. Taylor arrived in Arkansas County after 1825, making it impossible to know how much his taxable wealth had grown.

More typical of Arkansas County taxpayers was Achille Gordon, whose name was originally spelled Godin. In 1825 he was assessed for only 2 horses and 6 cattle, but by 1840 he owned 100 acres of land, 4 horses, and 16 head of cattle. James Young owned no land in 1825 and none in 1840, but his taxable horses increased from 2 to 3, his cattle herd from 30 to 40, and he acquired a slave. Samuel King had no taxable property in 1825, but owned a horse worth $100 in 1840. Eugene Jardelot was on the low end of economic success. He was among two dozen taxpayers in 1825 who had no taxable property, although one of his relatives owned 130 acres of land, 2 slaves, 4 horses, and 50 head of cattle. In 1840 Jardelot was still in Arkansas County and still without taxable property.

Overall, Arkansas County tax records tell us more about the growth of the regional economy than about the success of the individuals who were part of it. About 10 percent of the 1825 taxpayers appear on the tax list for 1840 and another 21 percent of the 1825 surnames match those of 1840. Given the fact that the county was much smaller in 1840, this is not surprising; many 1825 taxpayers were living in other counties in 1840 even if they had not moved. Moreover, it is clear that some of the 1840 taxable wealth was brought to Arkansas County by immigrants and thus is not a reflection of local productivity. For example, Notrebe was the only one among the 5 taxpayers who owned 20 or more slaves in 1840 who had been in Arkansas County in 1825.

A useful comparison can be made between Arkansas County and Washington County, located in the highland region of northwest Arkansas. Formed in part from Lovely's Purchase, Washington County was a popular destination for settlers arriving in the 1830s, even though it was located too far north for successful cotton cultivation. Although Benton County was formed from its northern portion in 1836, Washington County still had more than 7,000 inhabitants in 1840, making it by far the most populous of Arkansas counties. Arkansas as a whole had 2 persons per square mile in 1840, Arkansas County had only 1, but Washington County had more than 7. Agriculture in Washington County, as in most highland counties, was more diversified than in the lowlands. Washington was first among Arkansas counties in the production of oats, and it was second in the ownership of sheep, with something more than 1 per capita. Its farmers owned more horses and hogs than average and slightly fewer cattle. They grew slightly more corn than most counties and small but significant amounts of wheat and potatoes. Slaves were 12 percent of the population, less than half of the average for Arkansas as a whole.

The county seat of Washington County was Fayetteville, which was the location of a federal court and a land office. Archibald Yell, elected Democratic governor of Arkansas in 1840, lived there, and so did David Walker, a prominent Whig political leader. Although the town contained fewer than 500 persons in 1840, it was an important commercial center. Wealthy though he was, Frederick Notrebe seems to have been the only merchant of note in Arkansas Post. Washington County, on the other hand, had 25 or 30 businessmen whose collective invested capital ranked it along with Pulaski County and Crawford County among the top 3 centers of commercial activity in Arkansas. Shopkeepers in Washington County apparently bought goods wholesale from merchants in Van Buren on the Arkansas River in Crawford County, who themselves traded directly with Cincinnati and New Orleans. Given the additional commercial activity associated with Fort Smith across the river from Van Buren, western Arkansas seems to have had a business life largely independent of that in Little Rock.[25]

The diversity represented by counties like Arkansas and Washington makes it important to find some measure of economic growth for Arkansas as a whole. To do that, an attempt was made to locate the 987 sample tax-payers of 1840 5 years later in 1845. The lack of tax records for 8 counties in 1845 meant that only 739 were eligible for linkage and of them only 216 were actually matched with tax records in 1845. The 216 matched tax-payers had a mean taxable wealth that was 30 percent larger than that of the original 987 sample taxpayers of which they were a part, probably because the well-to-do are more visible in tax records than are the poor. If it is not perfectly representative, however, the matched group does provide some evidence as to what was possible within the Arkansas agricultural economy.[26]

Changes in taxable wealth for the group as a whole between 1840 and 1845 are summarized in Table 7. The most significant fact is the large increase in acres of land and in slaves, both of which grew more than twice as much as did the number of horses and cattle. Not shown in the table is the broadening of land ownership: 37 percent of the taxpayers owned land in 1840 and 50 percent in 1845. Despite the increase in taxable property, mean taxable wealth declined sharply because taxable property was assessed at lower rates in 1845 than in 1840 as the effects of the national depression that had begun in 1837 finally reached Arkansas.[27] Land was valued at 75 percent of the 1840 rate, slaves at 68 percent, horses at 59 percent, and cattle at 53 percent. Measured in constant 1840 values, taxable property increased 16 percent over the five-year period, an average annual rate of 3 percent.

TABLE 7

Wealth Mobility, 1840-1845

216 Matched Taxpayers

	1840	*1845*	*% Change*
Slaves	235	290	23.4
Acres	29,047	36,477	25.6
Cattle	1,452	1,587	9.3
Horses	545	608	11.6
Mean Taxable Wealth	$1,656	$1,365	-17.6

The experience of the matched taxpayers between 1840 and 1845 provides more evidence of economic growth in Arkansas. The rate of growth in taxable property is only about half of what is found in Arkansas County, but here the wealth of new settlers is not included. It was these 216 taxpayers who owned collectively 16 percent more property at the end of 5 years. Matched taxpayers, of course, do not tell us about the experience of the unmatched. It will become apparent in Chapter 5 that the distribution of taxable wealth was very unequal and that downward mobility may have been as significant as upward mobility. Nonetheless, Arkansas agriculture did provide significant economic opportunity.

∼

A testimonial to agricultural opportunity in Arkansas comes from Kirkbride Potts, who settled in Pope County in 1828 and gave his name to the modern town of Pottsville and to the Potts Tavern, which is now on the National Register of Historic Places. In 1830, Potts was a farmer who did not yet own his land, although he had a preemption claim to it. Still, he was a happy man with a wife he described as a "fine and agreeable woman" and also industrious. He was pleased at the large number of settlers moving into his area, most from Kentucky and Tennessee and some from Missouri, particularly since they bought corn at seventy-five cents a bushel and meat as well. After only two years, he was able to "raise more corn and wheat than we consume." Overall, he felt he had "a very good start in the world [with] more cattle than we use, [and our] hogs and beef are always fat without corn therefore we have the corn to sell." Writing to his sister in Bordentown, New Jersey, Kirkbride said that "nothing could induce me to live in jersey now for [I] can make more in one year here than I can there in five with the same labour."[28]

From its meager beginnings in 1820, Arkansas agriculture advanced steadily for two decades. By 1840 it was successful in a number of ways. Per capita production was high by the standards of nearby states. Cotton production was relatively small, but it was concentrated geographically and quite rewarding in those areas. Corn and hogs and cattle, on the other hand, must have provided a bountiful subsistence for almost everyone. Economic opportunity, in varying degrees, presented itself both to family farmers and to planters.

four

A Piece of the Territory

In January of 1831 the recently founded *Arkansas Advocate,* Little Rock's second newspaper, professed to be "astonished that so many of the sturdy and enterprising yeomanry of the older settled countries should *consent to wear out their lives as tenants* to some wealthy landlord; when by a single manly effort they might here lay the foundations of future independence, if not fortune, and become the lords of the soil they cultivate."[1] Despite its invidious attitude toward the East and its romantic tone, the argument was essentially correct. Land, the wellspring of economic opportunity in an agricultural society, was readily available in Arkansas. Abundant acreage could be purchased through the public land system, and it was usually possible to squat on the tract one wanted and to acquire the right to purchase it at a later date. Arkansas also offered alternatives to the auction sale of public land, exceptions that brought thousands of acres into private hands at bargain prices and were especially profitable for a narrow group of speculators and political insiders. Working the land was a form of opportunity but so also was buying and selling it.

~

The United States sold its land according to the system that originated in the Land Ordinance of 1785. The public domain was surveyed, divided into sections of 640 acres, and sold at public auction. Under the Land Act of 1800, purchasers were required to buy at least 320 acres at a minimum price of $2.00 per acre; paying, if they chose, only 5 percent down and the balance over 4 years. In 1820, just as land offices were opening up in Arkansas, the federal government eliminated the credit system but dropped the minimum price to $1.25 per acre and allowed the purchase of as little as 80 acres.[2] Congress also developed the concept of preemption to deal with the vexing problem of settlers who squatted on public land either before or after it was surveyed. The Preemption Act of April 12, 1814, legalized settlements made up to that time in Missouri Territory and gave individuals the right to purchase their holdings at the minimum price at some time in the future.[3]

The surveying of what became Arkansas began in 1815 with the running of the 5th Principal Meridian north from the mouth of the Arkansas River and a baseline west from the mouth of the St. Francis River. The first two land districts were established in 1818: Lawrence District, north of the base line, and Arkansas District, south of it. The first land sale in Arkansas Territory would have taken place in the fall of 1820 except that "forms and instructions" did not arrive in the mail on time. Thus settlers who had traveled several hundred miles to Arkansas Post to enter their preemption claims went home without doing so. Land offices finally opened about 1822 at Poke Bayou (later Batesville) and Little Rock.[4]

Hartwell Boswell, appointed to the Lawrence District in 1820, candidly acknowledged that "the duties of a register of the land office I am totally ignorant of." Nonetheless, he learned to do the job, and so did most of the other registers who recorded land entries and the receivers of public monies who collected the payments, in part because the General Land Office in Washington exercised vigorous oversight. Boswell, in fact, took up for the settlers, twice complaining to his superior that the surveyors working under William Rector, surveyor general in St. Louis, were saving choice land for themselves. Another sympathetic land official in Fayetteville in 1840 helped to correct the error when an illiterate man copied the wrong land entry numbers and wound up with a "range of flint ridges" instead of the farmland he wanted. Efficiency, of course, is a relative thing. Some measure of the speed at which business operated can be gauged from the statement of a receiver at the Washington, Arkansas, land office who wrote his superiors in the national capital that he was leaving to deposit money in the bank and would be "absent from four to six weeks."[5]

Land sales got off to a good start, with the purchase of more than twenty-two thousand acres in 1822, most of them bought with preemption rights earned by settlers who had been in Arkansas in April of 1814.

Purchases quickly fell off, however, and by the end of the decade only fifty-nine thousand acres had been sold.[6] National conditions were part of the problem. The Panic of 1819 and the ensuing depression slowed westward migration, and land sales fell off as a consequence. The ending of credit sales in 1820 was also a major blow to prospective purchasers. In Arkansas, land officials blamed lackluster sales on sluggish immigration and a shortage of cash. In 1823, one of them also pointed out that people were leaving the territory for better conditions in Texas. Three years later, however, a Batesville register offered a better explanation for the slow pace of land sales in the territory: "Persons desirous of purchasing hold back in expectation of securing [choice] lands . . . on better Terms from the French and Spanish Claimants and the Solders of the late war."[7] A great deal of land did become available in Arkansas as a result of Spanish claims and War of 1812 bounties. Each of these sources requires some discussion.

Spanish claims originated in the terms of the Louisiana Purchase, by which the United States agreed to protect the property rights of inhabitants in the territory under the government of Spain. Fulfilling this commitment, Congress in 1805 decided to confirm the title of bona fide grants made and settled prior to October 1, 1800, the date of the Treaty of San Ildefonso, under which Spain retroceded Louisiana to France, and de facto settlements existing before December 20, 1803, the day that the U.S. flag was raised over Louisiana. Arkansas claims under this legislation were heard by the Board of Land Commissioners for Louisiana Territory, which included the present states of Arkansas and Missouri. The board took evidence at St. Louis and in the various districts of the territory and issued a final report in 1812 that confirmed 1,340 claims, less than one-third of those it had considered. That same year Congress empowered Frederick Bates, one of the three land commissioners and the recorder of land titles in the new Missouri Territory, to rehear claims that had been rejected by the commission, a process that resulted in the approval of 1,756 more claims in Bates' report issued in 1816.[8]

The number of Spanish claims confirmed in what is now Arkansas reflected the limited nature of white settlement prior to the American occupation. The Board of Land Commissioners confirmed only 28 claims in 1812, 5 of them based on concessions from Spain and the rest on the basis of settlement. Bates approved 40 additional claims based on Spanish concessions and 77 based on settlement. As one might expect, most of the 145 tracts of land involved were located at or near Arkansas Post, with some on the Mississippi River and a few on the St. Francis, the White, and the Cache rivers. More than a third of the surnames on the 1798 census of

Arkansas Post show up on the list of successful claimants. Joseph Bogy, the leading farmer at the Post in the 1790s, was involved in 3 claims.

The amount of land granted was substantial. The first 28 claims approved averaged only 364 French arpents or about 309 acres. The 40 claims Bates approved on the basis of concessions were still smaller, averaging 293 acres each. The claims he approved on the basis of settlement were much larger, averaging more than 600 acres. Most of them were set at 640 acres and 3 of them totaled 5,600 arpents if the land could be surveyed within specified boundaries. There were a number of claimants who received more than 1 claim. Benjamin Fooy, a Dutchman who had been in the employ of Spain and who had settled at Fort Esperanza (later Hopefield and then West Memphis) in 1797, received 2,040 acres in 5 separate parcels. Sylvanus Phillips, for whom Phillips County would shortly be named, received 1,920 acres. In all, the 145 claims were rewarded with about 100 square miles of land, a substantial amount of real estate when one considers the limited amount of settlement that took place in Arkansas prior to the Louisiana Purchase.[9]

Some of the claims raise questions. Frederick Bates confirmed grants of 320 arpents allegedly made by the Spanish government to each of 8 infantrymen at Fort Esperanza in 1802. According to a document translated from Spanish by William Russell, a surveyor and land speculator, the soldiers then gave their sergeant, Augustin Grande, the power to dispose of the land for them and each of them certified that action by signing with an X. In 1819 Benjamin Fooy filed a deed of conveyance from Augustin Grande to himself for 4 of the 320-arpent parcels of land. The validity of signatures by 2 witnesses to the 1804 document was sworn to by Isaac Fooy and J. Henry Fooy, both of whom took their oaths before Benjamin Fooy, who was also a justice of the peace in Arkansas County.[10] Perhaps all this happened as the documents suggest, but the circumstances of the grants seem improbable, the process of validation lacks objectivity, and William Russell's involvement raises suspicion.

William Russell's name is on a large number of Spanish claims. Frederick Bates rejected most of Russell's more than 300 claims, confirming only one 640-acre tract in Arkansas for the speculator.[11] Still, Russell was assiduous in amassing acreage. For example, in 1813 he made an agreement with William McKenny, the owner of some 756 arpents (638 acres) of land along the Mississippi, by which Russell paid McKenny $100 and secured the right to all the land above 220 arpents (185.5 acres) for which he could secure confirmation. When Bates confirmed McKenny's claim to 640 acres, Russell earned 510 acres for his $100 plus expenses. In what seems to been a sharper deal, Russell bought 640 acres from Ebenezer Fulsome in July of 1816 with Fulsome unaware that the land had been confirmed to him. Similarly, Russell paid George Duvall $20 for 640 acres that had already been confirmed.[12]

An Arkansas settler named Chilo A. Moultier made serious allegations against Russell in a letter to the General Land Office in 1822. Moultier was protesting Bates' award of 640 acres to Elijah McKinney (whose relationship to William McKenny, above, is unknown) based on McKinney's residence at the mouth of Cache River before December of 1803. Moultier claimed that McKenny had not arrived before 1805, that he had hired someone else to make an improvement on the land, and that he then left Arkansas permanently. It apparently was not McKinney who had defrauded the United States, but William Russell, who had transformed himself from "a crafty Surveyor to become A crafty land Speculator." According to Moultier, Russell was the head of a "bandity" that had "got claims confirmed without the knowledge or intersession [sic] of those Pretended claimants in whose names they ware confirmed." He also suggested that only one of Silvanus Phillip's numerous claims could "stand the test of Public Justice" and that various public officials were a party to these "attrocious speculations."[13]

Moultier's view of Russell's character and mode of operations is echoed in a letter written in 1834 by William D. Ferguson of Crittenden County to Elijah Hayward, commissioner of the General Land Office. At issue were several tracts of land confirmed to John Grace and now sought by his heirs. Russell claimed the land, and, according to Ferguson, was "endeavouring to defraud" the heirs. Ferguson claimed to have known Grace well and that Grace had told him he had agreed to give Russell only 100 acres in return for Russell's patenting 2 tracts, 1 for 640 acres and 1 for 272 acres. Ferguson argued that "Russell took the advantage of Old John Grace's inability to do business—the Old Man being blind at the time as well as illiterate—by getting the Old Man to sign the deed for the 640 acres and the 100 acres instead of [only] the 100 acres."[14]

Among the claims that the commissioners turned down, the most important were those of the Winter family: Elisha, who sought 1,000,000 arpents of land, and his sons, William and Gabriel, each of whom wanted 250,000 arpents at first and then increased his request to 500,000. The latter amount made the claim of the 3 Winters come to somewhat more than 5 percent of the land area in modern Arkansas. According to the documentation in their claim, Elisha Winter was from Kentucky and had gone to New Orleans where he built a large rope walk that was subsequently destroyed by fire. Because of this loss and the friendship between them, in June of 1797, Baron de Carondolet, governor of Louisiana, granted Winter what his supporters referred to as "1,000 arpents square" and his sons each "500 arpens [sic] square" on the condition that they settle the land within a year. In the same document, Carondolet also gave 600 arpents each to 7 other men. The Winters then settled near Arkansas Post in 1798, bringing with them "slaves, horses, cattle, sheep, provisions, farming utensils, household and kitchen furniture, and a variety of other articles necessary for making a large farming establishment." Gabriel Winter, however, was still a minor when Louisiana became part of the United States.[15]

The commission ruled against the Winters in July of 1811, but, as usual, it did not explain its findings. The family pursued its case in Congress, and more than two decades later, the House Committee on Public Lands made a convincing case against the Winter claim. To begin with, there was the amount of land involved. The language of the grant gave to Elisha Winter, for example, *"mil arpanes de tierra quadrados,"* a thousand arpents of land squared. This was a confusing phrase because the arpent was usually understood as a surface measure analogous to an acre but 15 percent smaller. In Louisiana, however, the arpent was sometimes used as a linear measure of 192 feet, the length of one side of the surface arpent. The Winters argued that Elisha had been granted a thousand linear arpents by a thousand linear arpents or one million surface arpents. Although the committee did not do so, it was possible to argue that a thousand arpents squared meant simply a thousand surface arpents arranged in a square, as distinct, for example, from all of them lying along a river bank. This interpretation would allow Elisha a thousand arpents rather than a million and reduce William and Gabriel's amounts correspondingly.

This matter of interpretation, staggering in itself, was made worse for the committee by the fact that the original grant was never made available and the copy provided was not properly authorized. Moreover, there was no precedent in Spanish law or custom for a grant of the size that the Winters claimed. Finally, the committee did not believe that the grant was surveyed by Spanish authorities as it should have been. The Congressmen closed their report by offering the heirs of Elisha Winter two thousand acres of public land, an amount based on the actual settlement of Elisha and William.[16]

Military bounty lands were less complex than the Spanish claims and put more acreage into circulation. They originated during the War of 1812 when Congress offered 160 acres of the public domain to men who were willing to enlist for five years and then set aside six million acres for that purpose in the territories of Michigan, Illinois, and Louisiana. The Louisiana lands consisted of some two million acres located between the Arkansas and St. Francis Rivers in what became Missouri Territory and then Arkansas Territory. The survey there began in the fall of 1816, and the distribution of land began two years later. Many of the veterans who received their quarter sections of land, in Arkansas and elsewhere, seem to have sold them immediately to land speculators, and very few actually immigrated to the territory.[17] Meanwhile, under the law, bounty lands were exempt from local taxation for three years.

In October 1823, Acting Governor Robert Crittenden informed the legislature that the financial problems of Arkansas Territory would be easily solved the following year when the tax exemption for bounty lands expired and the territorial land tax of $1.50 per 100 acres could be extended to them. Crittenden believed that the territory could raise between $4,000 and $10,000, in his words, "a revenue principally raised from speculators and non-residents."[18] Obligingly, the legislature passed "An Act to Regulate the Collection of Taxes on Military Bounties," but it also included a provision that would enhance private interests in Arkansas Territory more than the public treasury. "Should the taxes not be paid . . . within sixty days" the county sheriff was to sell the land "at public sale" for the taxes after giving sixty days' notice of the sale "in some newspaper printed in this territory."[19]

The *Arkansas Gazette* did what it could to publicize the new law. Woodruff even offered to pay the taxes of anyone who would send him the money, explaining that he would make the payment in territorial script and profit by the exchange ratio. He also pointed out that individuals whose land was sold could redeem it under Arkansas law by paying the taxes and expenses within a year.[20] In April of 1824, he announced that the territorial government had obtained from the General Land Office a list of several thousand patents issued for Military Bounty Lands in Arkansas, most of which had apparently not been registered with local land offices because the owners wanted to avoid having their land put on the tax rolls.[21] Nonetheless, few owners of bounty lands paid the tax. Probably most of them never knew there was a tax. In October and November of 1824, tax sales were held in 5 separate Arkansas counties, and some 3,000 quarter sections of land were sold for a few dollars each instead of the $200 that the Land Office would have charged.[22]

In Arkansas County alone, 47,392 acres of military bounty land appeared on the tax rolls in 1825, about 80 percent as much land as the United States would sell in Arkansas during the entire 1820s. The bounty land had been purchased by 94 individuals, 67 of whom had brought 160 acres each. Nearly half the acreage, however, had been bought by 3 individuals, 1 of whom got 11,040 acres at the expense of the veterans. Only 5 of these new owners were residents of Arkansas County; the rest were apparently speculators who expected to resell the land to settlers. Aside from the veterans and the Government Land Office, the sale of bounty lands was good for everyone. The territory got the land on the tax rolls, and its citizens benefited from a significant bargain. Moreover, the sale was a windfall that spread itself more widely than many such events.[23]

In addition to the Spanish claims and the military bounty claims, there were other special opportunities that competed with the government's land sales. One of these was the New Madrid claims that originated as a means of compensating victims of the massive earthquakes of 1811–12 that devastated the landscape of a small portion of southeast Missouri and northwest Arkansas. In 1815 Congress passed a loosely written law providing that individuals who had lost at least one acre of land because of the earthquake could claim 160 acres of public land in the United States, and they could also sell their right to someone else. The New Madrid claims provided a windfall to most of the original claimants, some of whom obtained the compensation by fraud, and also to some speculators, who bought up the claims at low prices and then entered Arkansas Territory looking for choice land on which to locate. In one case, Charles Hempstead attempted to gain title to roughly the area of the present Hot Springs National Park with a New Madrid claim, but the United States refused to turn over what was already a well-known and valuable natural resource.[24] Many less spectacular claims succeeded, including one that helped to locate the capital of Arkansas Territory.

The movement of the territorial capital from Arkansas Post to Little Rock in 1821 was promoted by land speculators and accompanied by a vigorous battle between rival groups of speculators, one armed with New Madrid claims and the other with a preemption claim. In December 1819 James Bryan and William O'Hara, both of St. Louis, and their agent, Amos Wheeler, claimed the land that is now Little Rock based on their ownership of four New Madrid certificates. At the same time, William Russell argued that he was the rightful claimant because of a preemption right that had originated with William Lewis, a hunter who had lived near the future site of Little Rock for a few months in 1812. Apparently uncertain of his position, however, Russell offered to pay twenty-five thousand dollars for part of the New Madrid claim. The New Madrid forces not only rejected this offer, but they also threw Russell off what they were claiming as their land. Undaunted, Russell brought suit for wrongful trespass.[25]

The territorial legislature met in February 1820 and discussed moving the capital. Before them was a proposal by Wheeler for the New Madrid party, offering land and buildings to the territory if the capital were moved to Little Rock. Nonetheless, the house narrowly passed a motion to move to Cadron, a small community on the Arkansas River about twenty miles above Little Rock, and, when the council favored Little Rock, the issue was postponed. At its next session, in October, the house voted in favor of the Little Rock proposal six to three.[26] By that point a number of politicians held interests in the land on which the new capital would be located.

The widening of ownership appears to have begun on March 15, 1820, when William O'Hara sold Governor James Miller and Nathaniel Philbrook a twelfth of the New Madrid claim for eight hundred dollars.[27] Meanwhile, William Russell had attempted to firm up his preemption claim by taking title on January 7, 1820, to the Lewis preemption, for which he had paid one hundred dollars in silver the previous June. Russell bought the claim from Martha White, an heir of Elisha White, who had bought the claim to "Little Rock Bluff" from Lewis for ten dollars in 1814.[28] Alas for Russell, Elisha White apparently sold the claim before he died. In any case, in October Russell paid another two thousand dollars to Benjamin Murphy, William Trimble, and Townsend Dickinson for half of Lewis's preemption claim.[29] Murphy, who apparently registered the Lewis claim, dropped out of the picture at this point. William Trimble, an attorney whose brother was also the registrar of the Batesville Land Office, and Townsend Dickinson, a member of the legislative council, divided their share of the preemption rights with Robert Crittenden, territorial secretary and Arkansas's leading politician, with Henry W. Conway, receiver of public monies and an up-and-coming politician, with Joseph Hardin, speaker of the house, and with Robert C. Oden, an attorney and aspiring politician.

With the governor on one side of the competition, his aggressive and powerful secretary on the other, and the prize so readily divisible, an accommodation between the rival claimants was likely. The prospects of that were improved in June of 1821 when the Superior Court ruled on Russell's suit against the New Madrid group and found that Russell had been wrongfully ejected.[30] Finally, in November there was what Russell termed a "compromise." The preemptioners turned over seventeen lots to Chester Ashley, a young attorney from New York who came to Arkansas from St. Louis and managed the New Madrid claims, and Russell later purchased them back, in the process commingling the titles between the former adversaries. Ashley and Russell also bound themselves to support the legal right of each other, insuring that neither would challenge the deal in court.[31]

By the time that Russell and Ashley divided the spoils of speculation, the territorial legislature was already meeting in Little Rock. The lawmakers deliberated in a two-room log cabin, part of a community that included a dozen homes, a store, and several taverns and boarding houses.[32] The capital city would grow, however, and its real estate was potentially valuable. The Little Rock land deal is another illustration of how men with capital, legal skills, and political influence could make money out of territorial development. Political positions seem to have been used for private gain, but no laws were broken, and there were no apparent victims. The average citizen, however, was excluded from a process that provided significant gains for a favored few.

A final set of special land opportunities was the donation claims that arose out of the removal of the Cherokees from Arkansas. According to the Cherokee Treaty of May 1828, the Cherokees were moved west of a line drawn from Fort Smith to the southwest corner of Missouri. This line then became the northwest boundary of Arkansas Territory. Arkansas gained the Cherokee lands, but lost a large part of Lovely County, which had been organized in 1827 and had extended well to the west of the new boundary. An estimated 300 families lived on what was now Cherokee land west of the new territorial boundary and would have to move on; to compensate them for their losses, Congress provided each family a "donation" of 320 acres to be located anywhere on the public domain of the territory.[33]

Commissioner Graham of the General Land Office in Washington was concerned that the donation claims were susceptible to fraud. He wrote to the land offices at Little Rock and Batesville warning that a recipient of land under the act must be a head of family and over twenty-one years of age, must have been living in the area now belonging to the Cherokees when the law was passed on May 6, 1828, and must have been removed from the Cherokee lands since that time. He also pointed out that the only testimony required to prove these things was the same as that necessary for preemption claims, adding, "with these limited powers, and with the limited knowledge which you possess in relation to their number and character of the settlers on the ceded lands, it will be exceedingly difficult to guard against fraud and imposition."

According to several letters received later by Graham, the donation claims led to fraud that was both widespread and creative. Boys put pieces of paper in their shoes with 21 written on them so that witnesses could swear that they were "over 21," white men who lived with the Cherokees left their homes west of the line long enough to file for a donation of 320 acres and then returned to the Cherokee land, and boatmen who had traveled west of Fort Smith on the Arkansas River claimed that they were residents of the area. One estimate was that 1,500 to 2,000 donations would be requested from an area that was thought to contain only 300 families at best. Hopelessly, Graham wondered if the actual residents could be identified from the voting lists. Eventually, despite a warning from the commissioner, some individuals received more than one donation.[34]

Another aspect of the donation claims involved Ambrose Sevier, the elected delegate of the territory in Congress, William Woodruff, and Chester Ashley in what nearly became a major scandal. Sevier was in Woodruff's office on June 28, 1828, when a copy of the law providing for donations arrived. Reading the measure, which he had sponsored, Sevier learned that it inadvertently allowed the claimant to locate on any public land, whether improved or unimproved, and thus to take 320 acres that had been worked and built on but not yet purchased. One David Rorer happened into Woodruff's shop while this issue was being discussed by Sevier, Woodruff, and Ashley, and Rorer later claimed that Ashley wanted Woodruff to postpone the publication of the law so that those present might buy up donation claims and use them to locate on choice improvements.

On the basis of information from Rorer, a rumor circulated in the territory that Sevier, Woodruff, and Ashley were suppressing information to their own advantage and to the detriment of other settlers, a most damaging allegation to Sevier. In May of 1829, in the midst of Sevier's re-election campaign, Woodruff devoted a full page to statements related to the issue and explained in a letter of his own that there was no mention of suppressing publication of information. Instead, he, Sevier, and Ashley were simply concerned that persons with vulnerable improvements in the Little Rock area be informed verbally ahead of the general public so that they could protect themselves from losing their land. Joseph Henderson, however, admitted that he received a message from Ashley on that same day instructing him to buy two donation claims so that Ashley could protect some improvements of his own. Henderson went on to state that he purchased more claims, but that they were for himself.[35]

Sevier was elected—perhaps because the voters believed Woodruff, perhaps because his opponent, Richard Searcy, was also accused of speculation, or, most likely, because land manipulations were taken for granted. Chester Ashley was not yet running for office, but the ambiguous attitude toward his achievements is illustrated by a description made in 1831: "Ashley is under the character of a srude cunning atterny at law and a man of considerable tallence and a grate speculator in land for he owns a grat deal sucured by what is called in this country the lovely claimes . . ."[36]

As for the donation claims themselves, Woodruff, ever the local booster, exulted in February of 1829 that between 400 and 600 claims of 320 acres each had resulted from the donation law and that some $2,000 in new tax monies would come to the territory annually. Moreover, all this was done without the normal payment of about $200,000 to the federal government that would have served to "diminish the active capital of the Territory." Indeed, the savings may have been significant. Woodruff wrote to a private correspondent that military lands were hard to sell because "donations etc. . . . frequently enable immigrants to obtain good farms at little over 50 cts per acre."[37] The donation claims, like the New Madrid claims, the military bounty claims, and the Spanish claims, had put land into the hands of Arkansans without their having to go through the auction process or pay the $1.25 per acre minimum price.

~

Finally, there are the Bowie claims, which may usefully be discussed in detail, not because they involved a great deal of acreage, but because they illustrate so vividly the bold fraudulence of the land business in Arkansas and the environment in which it flourished. The story begins in 1824 as the Spanish claims entered a new phase when Congress gave the Superior Court of Arkansas jurisdiction over any new cases. No claims were brought immediately, but by April of 1826, the Superior Court had confirmed 10,725 acres of land originally granted by the Spanish government and now in the hands of citizens of the territory.[38]

In December of 1827, the court heard and acted on what would become known as the Bowie claims. George Graham, commissioner of the General Land Office, first learned of these in a letter from the Little Rock land office, which mentioned that the Arkansas court had confirmed some 50,000 acres of land at its last session. The local land office feared that as the recipients put their new property up for sale, the demand for U.S. government land would be further depressed. As the new claims were processed, Graham became suspicious about their validity. He discussed the matter with Attorney General William Wirt, corresponded with the U.S. district attorney in Arkansas, Sam Roane, and finally decided to have a special investigator examine the documentation of the new claims.[39]

Graham's investigator was a New Orleans land expert named Isaac T. Preston, who visited Little Rock and filed a most interesting report in October 1829. As Preston explained, the Superior Court of Arkansas had confirmed 117 claims between December 19 and 24, 1828, and left pending another 7 cases for its next meeting. All of these 124 claims, which did involve about 50,000 acres of land, were based on the testimony of 3 men. In all cases, the depositions were "substantially, and in general literally," the same. Preston found it absurd that the deponents would have known personally all these men who were supposed to have been in Arkansas between 1785 and 1798. Clearer evidence of fraud, however, was the signatures of Spanish governors, Miro and Gayoso, which to Preston's trained eye were obvious forgeries. He also pointed out that certain Spanish words, *tierra* and *ordinaria* for example, were uniformly misspelled throughout the Spanish documents, which were supposedly written by a variety of Spanish officials. Finally, the claims themselves, allegedly made separately by 124 different people, were in the handwriting of no more than 4 and probably only 2 individuals. Summing up, Preston declared that "the tout ensemble, to any eye accustomed to see ancient Spanish documents, would produce the instant and undoubted conviction of their falsity."

After discussing the significance of the crime, Preston pointed out that the beneficiaries could locate their claims in small amounts and anywhere in Arkansas. As he put it, they could "pick the territory" for choice land. While developing some emotion, he defined the issue as whether the United States "can be successfully plundered by the most unparalleled forgery, perjury, and subornation," or, putting it another way, whether "great actors may roll in wealth, whilst an honest man and woman may labor their life-time in these woods to acquire a quarter section of land for their children, and perhaps finally fail because they could not accumulate $200." Preston did not speculate as to the identity of the "great actors" he condemned. He did refer to the "Bowie Claims," as they were apparently known in Arkansas. He also argued, however, that "men of the deepest thought, as well as the Bowies, are embarked in this business."[40]

With his report, Preston sent a list of the 124 claims and the amount of land involved in each. He also included a copy of the depositions in one case, *Valire Leprete v. United States*. In that case, one of the deponents was John Heberard, who swore that he had been a Spanish official between 1789 and 1791 and again in 1797, that he was familiar with the signatures of Gayoso and Miro, and that he knew of the manner in which they disposed of land. The record of land grants by the governors, he believed, had been destroyed. He did not know the claimant Leprete personally, but testified to his belief that the documentation associated with the claim was genuine. Heberard claimed to know well the Strawberry River region where the grant was located and to have no doubt that the grant had been made there. The second deponent, David Devore, swore to the validity of the signatures and also to the authenticity of Heberard. Finally, Lemual Masters also attested to the signatures.[41] In addition to his other criticism, Preston pointed out that the record of grants by Spanish officials not only existed, but also that he had it in his possession.

In the hands of Commissioner Graham, Preston's report brought action. Congress in early 1830 extended the duration of the Superior Court's jurisdiction over Spanish claims and instructed it to review the Bowie claims. U.S. Attorney Roane secured depositions from experts in New Orleans indicating that the Bowie documents were counterfeited and that the governors' signatures were forged. During May and June of 1830, the Superior Court accepted bills of review filed by Roane. This was done over the objections of prominent Arkansas attorneys Chester Ashley and Robert Crittenden, who were acting on behalf of the claimants with confirmed land.[42]

Eventually, one case resulted. Joseph Stewart claimed title to land that he had purchased from John J. Bowie. Bowie was the brother of Jim Bowie and had lived in the New Orleans area for a time while he, Jim, and their brother Rezin had engaged in the smuggling of slaves. At the time of the Bowie claims, John J. was involved in property transactions in Chicot County, Arkansas, and he later lived in Helena, Arkansas. Bowie's title was based on the confirmed Spanish claim of one Bernardo Sampeyreac. The Superior Court now ruled that Sampeyreac was a fictitious person and that no legitimate title ever existed. Stewart was out of luck. He carried the case to the United States Supreme Court, which upheld the Arkansas decision. With this ruling as a precedent, the remaining claims were invalidated by the Superior Court without further litigation. In each instance, it ruled that the original claimant was not a real person.[43] A number of third-party purchasers lost out in this process, but the United States did eventually award them preemption rights to the land they thought they had bought.[44]

No one was punished for the crimes that had been committed. No charges were brought against the perpetrators of the fraud, perhaps because the Superior Court allowed the individuals who filed the claims to withdraw the original, forged documents before they could be seized as evidence in criminal proceedings. A coverup of sorts began in January of 1830 when the *Arkansas Gazette* published a letter from Ambrose Sevier, the territorial delegate in Washington indicating that Congress would force a review of the claims despite his opposition. Sevier believed it would have been better for Arkansas if the claims had remained in Louisiana, since "they have, although unjustly, injured the character of our Courts, our District Attorney, and our citizens generally." A month later William Woodruff took the same tack in a more forceful manner. Wrote the editor, "If there has been fraud committed, . . . it is not chargeable upon Arkansas, but upon the Bowies of Louisiana. . . . Arkansas has no agency in it."[45]

U.S. Attorney Roane knew better. Defending himself against a charge of laxness in not challenging the claims when first presented, Roane claimed he could not investigate them because he lacked money and a knowledge of Spanish. In a later letter, however, he gave a better reason and inadvertently destroyed the idea of Arkansas's innocence. "There is in Arkansas a powerful interest in favor of those claims. The property in them is widely diffused through every part of the country. . . . Even before the confirmation, the persons who were the main actors had sold and ramified the interest in them so extensively, that the community were urged by self interest to see them confirmed."[46]

And who were the "main actors"? Roane asserted that the claims "were manufactured in Louisiana and brought to Arkansas by John J. Bowie or James Bowie, and their agents." William S. Fulton, the territorial secretary, wrote President Jackson that "Ashley[,] Crittenden and Bowie" held all these claims, and he was apparently right. At the National Archives is a document titled "Locations of the Decrees of the Superior Court of the late Territory of Arkansas under the Act of 1824 which decrees were subsequently Reversed by the said Court and provisions made by Congress for the relief of bona fide purchasers." Dating apparently from the 1840s, this list includes 65 of the original Bowie grants, giving the fictitious name of the original confirmee and then the names of the first assignee and later assignees. The first assignees include only 3 persons. John J. Bowie is listed with 25 claims totaling 10,047 acres, Chester Ashley is listed with 22 claims totaling 9,218 acres, and Robert Crittenden is listed with 9 claims amounting to 3,583 acres.[47]

While running for the U.S. Senate in 1844, Chester Ashley defended his involvement with the Bowie claims on the grounds that he and Crittenden, who were legal partners, were simply acting as representatives for John J. Bowie, that they each received "five or six" claims in compensation, and that they were "innocent victims." As we have seen, Ashley received many more than five or six claims. Moreover, among his papers is a list of his expenses in the case, drawn up so that they could be paid by Bowie. In addition to court fees for each claim, there is a payment of five hundred dollars to the witnesses Devore and Masters, a variety of other expenses related to travel and lodging for all three witnesses, and the costs for at least one trip Ashley made to Louisiana.[48] Ashley had been involved in legal affairs relating to Arkansas land for about six years when the Bowie claims were first advanced. It is difficult to believe that a man of his intelligence and experience could be so closely involved in so fraudulent an activity and not be aware of what was happening.

The involvement of Ashley and Crittenden also makes it easier to understand the Bowie claims in general. Ashley was a major figure in the political faction headed by Ambrose Sevier, the territorial delegate. Crittenden was the territorial secretary in 1828 and head of a faction that opposed Sevier. Assuming that they were willing to cooperate, which seems apparent, Ashley and Crittenden were in a position to insure that the claims were well received by Arkansas officials. Thus, the Superior Court approved the cases quickly when they were first presented and later allowed the evidence of fraud to be removed. Therefore, Roane did not seriously question the claims until he was pushed to do so, and the only name he referred to was John J. Bowie, who was not a political insider in Arkansas. William Woodruff, who joined Sevier in proclaiming the innocence of Arkansas, was Ashley's political ally and best friend.

The Bowie claims probably did originate in Louisiana, where Spanish claims were routinely manipulated, but their near success in Arkansas Territory was due to local politics and customs. Ashley and Crittenden were in a position to wield important influence, a fact that explains why Bowie would have sought them out. On the other hand, the judges of the Superior Court, and probably a number of other prominent individuals, among them Sevier and Woodruff, were willing to accept an obvious fraud and to protect its perpetrators. Despite the public statements that acknowledge the possibility of illegal activity, one has the sense that taking land away from the federal government was not seen in Arkansas as very reprehensible. This viewpoint was part of a larger attitude, which we have seen relative to the Indians and which we will come upon again, that citizens who ventured into a territory deserved to have what was there and that the role of the federal government should be to help them get it.

~

During the decade of the 1830s, the land business became more active in Arkansas and much more uniform. The absence of special land situations such as existed in the 1820s encouraged more people to buy at the public auctions. Moreover, a general preemption law passed in 1830 allowed settlers on the public domain to preempt 160 acres if the claim was made by May 29, 1831. James Miller, the first governor of Arkansas, had called for such a law back in 1821 because of the number of squatters in the territory, and the situation was unchanged a decade later. The *Arkansas Gazette* touted the 1830 measure as "a most important law for Arkansas" and, when the deadline neared, reported that "a great number of our citizens" had filed claims for preemption.[49]

Both immigration and the sale of land in Arkansas during the decade of the 1830s were closely linked to the general phenomenon of American expansion to the West. The price of cotton and other agricultural commodities rose, and pioneers migrated to unoccupied public land in all the states and territories where it existed. Land sales increased dramatically in Arkansas Territory, but the same was true of Missouri and Louisiana; it was also true of Florida, Alabama, and Mississippi; and it was true as well of Ohio, Indiana, Illinois, and Michigan Territory. Indeed, the dramatic increase in the annual sale of public land in Arkansas during the 1830s correlates almost perfectly with the increase in the sale of public land generally. The peak year for Arkansas was 1836, when the territory became a state and when nearly a million acres of public land were sold; that same year the United States sold about twenty million acres of public land, by far its highest total as well. Land sales in Arkansas were related to a general phenomenon of expansion rather than to the particular allurements of statehood.[50]

In any event, the land business boomed. In 1832 the General Land Office supplemented its local offices at Little Rock and Batesville with two new ones at Washington and Fayetteville. Arkansas Territory also got its own surveyor general, ending a long period in which local affairs were supervised from St. Louis. In 1834 another land office was opened at Helena to deal with land along the Mississippi River. At the end of that year, lots were auctioned for the town of Fayetteville, which was to be located on a quarter section of land given by Congress to Washington County for its county seat. In advertising the sale, the county commissioners struck a tone of pride and optimism. The site was "on a beautiful eminence," providing a view of "blue hills and mountains" and "prairies." It was "surrounded with a rich, fertile, and healthy country, already densely populated, and well supplied with never-failing springs of the best water." In their view, it "bids fair to become one of the most flourishing inland towns west of the Mississippi."[51]

Washington County was flourishing, but the busiest land offices were those at Little Rock, Washington, and Helena, which covered southern Arkansas where cotton could easily be grown and where the Mississippi River, Ouachita River, and the newly opened Red River provided transportation to markets. Late in 1834, the *Arkansas Gazette* noted that for several months "vast numbers of movers many of them with large drives of negroes" had passed through Little Rock headed south for the Red River country. A land sale held at Washington, the Hempstead County town that housed the Red River Land District, in December took in more than any previous auction and saw lands go for as high as twelve dollars per acre. Behind the high prices was the success of Captain Shreve at "tearing away and removing the obstructions" that impeded navigation of the river. A year later the immigration was still going on as one of the territory's garden spots was finally fulfilling its potential.[52]

The extraordinary land boom may have led to increased speculation and corruption. George Featherstonhaugh visited the land auction at Washington, Arkansas, and shortly afterwards he wrote at length about American avarice in general and land speculation in particular. Speculators, he claimed, were successful in part because they were able to "place one of their number as principal person in the land-office in the district to be operated in." By using this inside influence, these unscrupulous persons could usually manipulate, intimidate, and cheat "the industrious and unsuspecting settler" out of the best tracts. Another sort of fraud was described by a writer who signed himself "Hamlet" and claimed to live on the south side of Red River. He warned the *Gazette* that fictitious claims were being sold to the land around him. These he described as supposedly "from Mexico but said to be of Bowie manufacture."[53]

Whatever the conditions under which it happened, the structure of landholding in Arkansas in 1840 was remarkably changed from what it had been ten years earlier. The sale of public land during the 1820s amounted to 2.3 acres for each white person in the state in 1830; during the 1830s the population grew markedly, but land sales increased still more, and by 1840 the total amount of land sold per white capita amounted to 31.7 acres. An average household with 6.3 white persons, therefore, would have owned 200 acres if the land had been distributed equally. Of course, it was not.

The actual structure of land ownership in 1840 was markedly unequal. Only a third of the state's taxpayers owned any land at all. The other two-thirds, however, were probably neither tenants nor poverty-stricken. Many taxpayers, as will become clear, were young men living in someone else's household. Other nonowners were squatters who felt little pressure to purchase land, protected as they were by preemption and the still-unsettled condition of the state. There were only two people per square mile in Arkansas in 1840, and a vast amount of public domain was not yet sold. The high level of landlessness was probably also a function of the increased immigration of the late 1830s. For whatever reason, landholding was slightly more prevalent in the lowlands, which contained 40 percent of the sample taxpayers and 45 percent of those who owned land.

The distribution of landholdings is given in Table 8. Thirty-nine percent of the landowners in our sample owned fewer than one hundred acres, and another 49 percent owned between one hundred and five hundred acres. Members of these groups were as likely to be found in the highlands as in the lowlands. Landowners with large holdings, for Arkansas at least, of five hundred acres or more were more apt to be located in the lowlands. Large farms, along with large cattle herds and most of the slaves in the territory, were part of the developing plantation economy that was a lowland phenomenon.

TABLE 8
Landholdings by Acres and Section

	1–99		100–199		200–499		500–		Total	
	N	%	N	%	N	%	N	%	N	%
Lowlands	56	17	32	10	30	9	27	8	145	45
Highlands	72	22	47	14	47	14	14	4	180	55
Total	128	39	79	24	47	23	41	12	325	100

~

The public land system of the United States affected Arkansas Territory in two very important ways. Its greatest significance was to transfer public resources to private owners who could use them in a productive manner, thus improving the lives of individual settlers and contributing to the growth and development of the country. A secondary function of the land system, presumably unintended by the lawmakers who designed the system, was to promote the rapid economic mobility of individuals with the special skills necessary to manipulate or defraud the government to their special advantage. The territorial public must have learned, if it did not already know, about the high profits available in land speculation in March of 1836 when Chester Ashley took out a front-page advertisement in the *Arkansas Gazette* addressed to "Planters and Capitalists." Stimulated, one supposes, by the continuing boom in land sales and the approach of statehood, Ashley placed on the market 35,281 acres of land owned by himself in cotton-rich Chicot County and on the Arkansas River south of Little Rock.[54]

Ashley's princely acreage testified to the large opportunity that had existed in acquiring Arkansas land. Thus while the unequal nature of land ownership in Arkansas was a reflection of American society and of the disparate resources that settlers brought with them, it was also molded by the nature of local circumstances.

five

Women Settlers

The Bear State image of Arkansas was as unkind to white women as it was to white men. Washburn's "Arkansas Traveler," for example, shows the squatter's wife standing on the dirt floor of the ramshackle log cabin with a pipe in her mouth, hardly an argument for domesticity as it was known in the nineteenth century. On the other hand, the woman was making do. Her hair was drawn back and in place, she wore a dress with sleeves and a tie at the waist, she held a frying pan in her hand, apparently getting ready to cook. She also seemed to be keeping an eye on the four small children standing outside as well as on an older girl who was combing her hair inside the cabin.

Written accounts of white women in Arkansas Territory are often less even-handed than Washburn's painting, describing them as crude woods women and careless homemakers, ill suited for economic advancement and apparently uninterested in it. They were perfect mates for their shiftless, backwoods husbands; in Grady McWhiney's parlance, they were cracker wives for cracker men. If these women were all there were in Arkansas, agricultural success would be hard to explain.

There are other images of settler women, however. One of these is best termed traditional, recalling as it does the colonial past. Arkansas women raised very large familes as many women did in the seventeenth and eighteenth centuries, probably in response to the availability of land. They also exercised a significant amount of economic responsibility in place of their husbands, another trait of colonial households. This traditional role made territorial women highly functional in an agricultural society and helps to explain Arkansas's economic progress.

The degree to which Arkansas women were different from other women of the early republic ought not to be exaggerated. Despite their location far from the centers of feminine values and fashion, they do not seem to have been isolated from those things. They were also involved with religious affairs and with the fellowship of other women. Like the men they accompanied, settler women did not reject the culture of the East; rather, they attempted to recreate it on more favorable terms for themselves.

~

Henry Schoolcraft, the young traveling geologist, condemned the pioneer society of Lawrence County in 1818 as "not essentially different from that which exists among the savages." It was an unfair judgment, and in making it Schoolcraft also seemed to assign women more than an equal share of blame. The cause of this alleged primitivism, he believed, was hunting, an activity or a vocational choice of men. He found, however, virtues in "the hardy, frank, and independent hunters": a kind of noble savagery that softened his other criticism of them. Schoolcraft was implicitly more critical of the women. In his enumeration of the deficiencies of Lawrence County culture, the geologist listed many things that the early American republic believed were the responsibility of women: "manners, morals, customs, dress, . . . schools, religion, and learning." Nor did he soften this judgment with any kind words for the female settlers, even though one of them had fed him an excellent meal of hot cornbread with butter, honey, and milk. Schoolcraft was able to appreciate the activity of men in a frontier environment but not that of women; to them, he applied only the standards of eastern society.[1]

Governor James Miller, who did not bring his own wife to Arkansas, had a similar perspective. While writing to her in New Hampshire about social life in Arkansas Post in 1820, he was unable to appreciate female behavior that was different from that to which he was accustomed. "Society," he wrote, "is very uncultivated." On the weekends men and women attended parties where they danced and played cards through the night. With the exception of "one young lady, . . . the ladies are married, from twenty to seventy-five years of age." The women all brought their children, some of them "young sucking children," whom "they nurse as unconcerned as at home in their nursery." At "daylight . . . each of the fair sex saddles her pony, mounts, and trudges home. The men generally hold on longer at the card table." These festivities were similar to those enjoyed by other French settlers in the Mississippi Valley, but very different from those of the northeastern United States.[2]

Another New Englander, Hiram Whittington of Boston, was shocked by Arkansas women in general. As he traveled up the Arkansas River in December 1826, the twenty-one-year-old Whittington stayed in cabins where he spent the night in the same room with both the male and female residents. Embarrassed that the women refused to leave so he could change, Whittington slept in his "pantaloons." At Little Rock he found the women "ugly as sin" and noted that both young and old among them attended parties where they danced all night to the music of a "violin." Girls would occasionally stop dancing, unpin their clothes, and scratch at ticks. Scornfully, he wrote home that two "French ladies" went walking with raccoons that functioned as "lap dogs."[3]

During the next year, Whittington complained that there were so few women in Little Rock that they "were snatched up by the men like a piece of meat." He joked that "black girls" were all that were available and that the height of his ambition was to marry a "Cherokee squaw." In December of 1830, he described an outstanding example of the crude and unrefined Arkansas woman. Rebecca Barkman was married to Jacob, a merchant and landowner of Blakelytown, now Arkadelphia, on the Ouachita River, one of the wealthiest men in the territory. She was about fifty years old and weighed about two hundred pounds. In addition, wrote Whittington, she "smokes a dirty pipe . . . never had a bonnet on her head in her life . . . [and instead wears] a handkerchief tied round her head, and a bearskin shawl over her shoulders." Finally, "she has a very awkward way of boxing her husband's ears when he displeases her."[4]

"A Traveler" who wrote in the *Arkansas Gazette* was disgusted by the housekeeping habits of Arkansas women. He pointed out that the territorial poor either owned land or had access to it and that their "carelessness and bad management tend much more than their poverty to make their houses disagreeable." He blamed men for the fact that many houses were poorly constructed or in disrepair, but directed many other criticisms at women. After claiming to appreciate simple food, he disdained a breakfast of "soft frothy butter, a large loaf of bread that has sweated in the oven all night, and milk about equal." Some of the settlers "are so dirty that their houses smell unpleasant, and their victuals are disgusting." When sweeping was done, it was often done when food was on the table, and sometimes the dust raised was thick enough to make breathing difficult.[5]

Finally, there is the experience of the English-born George Featherstonhaugh, who traveled through Arkansas in the mid 1830s. On the upper White River he stayed overnight with a Widow Harris, who lived with her children in a double log cabin. She offered the travelers only "bad fried bits of pork, with worse bread, and no milk." Mrs. Harris surprised Featherstonhaugh by sleeping in a bed next to his and by asking for tobacco the next morning. Still, he felt the Harrises "were an amiable and good family of people, and not without the means of living comfortably if they only knew how to set about it." As he continued his journey, Featherstonhaugh became accustomed to sleeping in the same room with his female hosts, but he could still be shocked. Like Whittington, he met Rebecca Barkman and was taken aback. She "chewed tobacco, . . . smoked a pipe, . . . drank whiskey, and cursed and swore as heartily as any backwoodsman."[6]

Not all women were like these. Featherstonhaugh seemed happy with Mary Jane Conway, wife of the surveyor-general and later Governor James Conway, and with the accommodations at the Conway home at Magnet Cove near Hot Springs. He was also handsomely entertained by Laura Cross, "a lady-like and agreeable woman," who lived near the Red River with her husband, Judge Edward Cross. Friederich Gerstäcker, the German traveler, was complimentary to many of the Arkansans he met including one "family not to be surpassed in worth and amiable qualities in any part of the world. An old man . . . still strong and hearty . . . a noble-looking matron . . . a young and pretty woman of the neighborhood . . . three stout, blooming youths."[7]

Despite these exceptions, contemporary observers usually wrote about Arkansas women in terms of their crude lifestyles and rude behavior. Certainly there was some truth to these criticisms, but they also seem exaggerated and unbalanced, reflecting the prejudices and pretensions of the writer as much as the circumstances. They are also similar to the comments that northerners made about the South in general as they described what Grady McWhiney calls "cracker culture."[8] Whatever their bias, these descriptions left out many things that probably seemed uninteresting at the time. Among these was the demography of white society.

~

The American family began to drop in size in the late eighteenth century. In 1800, women who were married throughout their reproductive years gave birth to an average of about seven children; by 1840, that figure had dropped to six, and by 1900 it was down to four. The change occurred first in the Northeast within a commercial economy that was moving toward industrialism; only slowly did it affect the agricultural South. Historian Daniel Scott Smith has argued that smaller families were linked to increasing female autonomy. Women wanted to have fewer children in order to have more time and energy for themselves, and they convinced their husbands to participate in family planning and birth control.[9]

Meanwhile, Arkansas women were the most prolific in the nation in 1840. The refined birth rate, calculated as the number of children under ten for every one thousand women aged sixteen through forty-four, was higher in Arkansas than any other state or territory and a startling 43 percent higher than in the United States as a whole.[10] The effect of this fertility on Arkansas households is illustrated in Table 9.

TABLE 9

Composition of Arkansas Households in 1840,
Age Categories of Women by Mean Number of Children and Men,
and by Size of Household

	Children		Men		Household Size
	0–9	10–19	20–49	50–	
One Woman					
Age 15–19 (N=45)	1.1	.5	1.2	.1	3.9
Age 20–29 (N=139)	2.6	.6	1.3	.0	5.5
Age 30–39 (N=93)	3.4	2.2	1.4	.1	8.0
Age 40–49 (N=50)	2.3	2.8	1.1	.3	7.4
Age 50– (N=21)	.7	2.6	.9	.7	5.6
More Than One					
Woman (N=40)	2.2	2.4	1.5	.5	8.8
No Woman (N=24)	.2	.5	1.0	.3	1.9
All Households					
(N=412)	2.3	1.6	1.3	.2	6.3

Note: Females 15 to 19 years old are counted as children except when there is no older female in the household. In three households where there were two females 15 to 19 years old and no older woman, one is counted as a woman and one as a child.

Arkansas women seem to have married early, to have begun bearing children immediately, and to have cared for children throughout most of their lives. In 11 percent of the sample households, the oldest female was between fifteen and nineteen. Some of these women were probably single and living with widowed fathers, but most appear to have been married and on their own.[11] Well over half of these households contained a child under ten years old. More than half of all the households belonged to a woman in her twenties or thirties, and these illustrate the phenomenon of high birth rate. Women in their twenties lived with an average of three children, most of them under ten. Women in their thirties lived with five or six youngsters, three or four of them under ten. The number of children decreases with older women, but even those in their fifties had an average of three children in their households, one of whom was sometimes under ten.

Women were also a minority among adults. In 1840, women of child-bearing age made up only 17.3 percent of the white population in Arkansas, a lower figure than in any other state or territory and 3.6 percent lower than in the United States as a whole.[12] In terms that probably would have meant more to the settlers, there were three white men for every two white women in Arkansas. Yet these extra men seldom lived alone; only 6 percent of all the households were without a woman. Instead, a significant number of households contained more than one man. In the 349 households with one women in her twenties or thirties, there were a total of 520 adult males, 171 more than one would expect in nuclear families. The identity of these men is not given by the census; probably, however, many were relatives of the head of household and his wife.

The demographic characteristics of white society in Arkansas were similar to those of other American frontiers of the nineteenth century. Despite the mythology of the lone frontiersman, women and children were much in evidence at the edges of expansion, and single males were normally attached to someone's family. The high birth rate in these areas contrasted not only with the commercial Northeast but also with older agricultural areas. Exactly why frontier families had more children is not clear. One argument is that children were of economic use on the farm. This is a compelling idea, except that it fails to explain why the birth rate was lower in older agricultural regions where the labor of the youngsters would be equally beneficial. The availability of land may also have encouraged large families by reassuring parents that children would have economic opportunities of their own. This seems reasonable, but evidence is lacking. On somewhat sounder ground is the hypothesis advanced by historian James E. Davis, who claims that the possibilities of economic subsistence made the frontier attractive to large families. After having demonstrated that households were larger on the southern frontier than in similar areas in the North, Davis argues that the South was "more agrarian . . . and it retained its agrarian nature longer," making subsistence easier. Thus

Arkansans raised "large families without dire consequences" because of the corn, pork, and cattle that came so readily to hand.[13]

The fertility of Arkansas women underlines the agricultural nature of Arkansas society. It also gives them more in common with colonial women who were pregnant every other year than with their family-planning contemporaries in the Northeast. As has been suggested, that traditionalism is strengthened by an examination of the women's role in the agricultural economy.

~

Large families and large households suggest a family that is functioning as an independent social and economic unit. In fact, southern families were more apt to migrate in single households than were northern households, and the isolation of the journey and the new home may have made parents want to increase the size of their families.[14] Moreover, when households were economic units, as they were on farms or plantations, women were involved in economic activity more than they were in situations in which the man of the house went off somewhere to work. That circumstance, quite common in the eighteenth century, was also apparent in territorial Arkansas. Arkansas women often functioned as "deputy husbands," to use a term coined by historian Laurel Thatcher Ulrich to describe women of colonial New England who advised their husbands on economic matters and acted in place of them when necessary. These women combined household management and child care with a significant involvement in bread winning; the dual roles were made possible by the fact that "the home was the communication center of family enterprise if not always the actual place of work."[15] Women were also sometimes more directly involved in farm management.

About 2 percent of Arkansas households were headed by women.[16] For Mary Roberts of Conway County, a woman in her thirties, this meant having responsibility for two hundred acres of land, three taxable horses, and six taxable cattle in addition to five children, one of whom was under five years old. A woman named Mason Roberts settled a claim north of the Arkansas River in 1827 with six children and three servants. She farmed seven acres there until the land was given to the Cherokees, and then she relocated in Crawford County. Elizabeth Moss operated a farm on Mulberry Creek that a land official described as "in the greatest state of improvement." Mrs. Sarah Embree of Jefferson County, "an elderly and very worthy lady," was described by the *Arkansas Gazette* as "one of the best practical cotton planters in the Territory." In 1834 her cotton sold for a penny a pound higher than any other in the New Orleans market at that time.[17]

Polly Hillhouse of Lawrence County left a record of her effectiveness as a farm manager. When Eli Hillhouse died in 1820, he left Polly "all my stock consisting of horses, cattle, sheep, and hogs together with all my farming tools[,] household & kitchen furniture[,] also the use of my improvement and right of preemption together with all money notes and accounts . . . until the youngest children comes of age that she may be able to raise and educate them in a suitable manner." It was a wise decision. At Eli's death the estate was valued at $724; when Polly died in 1834, she owned $1,761 worth of property, including 219 acres of land, 2 slaves, comfortable household furnishings, and $522 in cash.[18] The annual rate of increase in taxable wealth under Polly's stewardship was 6.5 percent.

Another early farm wife of Lawrence County was Margaret Criswell, whose husband, Andrew, died in 1819, about the time Schoolcraft claimed the area was inhabited by savage-like hunters. Since he left no will, Criswell's estate was inventoried and sold. His wife, however, first selected out the one-third portion that was her dower right. Among the things chosen by Margaret Criswell were furniture such as a feather bed and bed-clothes, four "old chairs," two dishes and five plates, and "the pewter." She also claimed a significant amount of equipment for household production: a cotton wheel, a flax wheel, a loom, two churns, and a tub. Among the livestock, she took a cow, a calf, a heifer, and fifteen young hogs. Finally, Margaret also felt she would need two hoes, a log chain, an iron wedge, a plough, a grindstone, and three axes. She was a very practical women who knew her way around a farm.[19]

More evidence about the women of Lawrence County comes from the twenty-four wills filed by married men between 1819 and 1836.[20] Neither a large nor a scientific sample, the Lawrence County wills do provide useful insights into the nature of frontier society and the role of women in that society. It was clearly an unlettered culture; only a third of the testators were able to sign their own wills. With the exception of one doctor, all the men were farmers. While some of them were quite poor, seven of the testators owned slaves, suggesting that as a group they were more wealthy than their neighbors.

The overwhelming impression from these wills is that they were written in order to enlarge the property rights of the widow, usually so that she would be able to take care of the children, functioning as a "deputy husband." Without a will, a married man's property would be divided, and his wife would receive one-third as her dower if there were children and one-half if there were none.[21] Only one man specified that the wife should receive one-third of the estate. Another will provided that the widow should have the use of two slaves and be able to live on the farm during her lifetime. Henderson White, the doctor, gave his wife her one-third and also a slave girl, a horse, a saddle and bridle, and two sets of silver spoons. Three other wills are ambiguous about whether the widow's portion is more than her dower share. In the remaining eighteen wills, the husband enlarged upon his wife's dower rights in significant ways.

Nine of the twenty-four wills provided the widow with the use of most of the property during her lifetime; the male testators obviously believed that their wives could cope with that responsibility. John Tyler, Jr., who died in 1823, was very explicit, giving "the whole of his property after his just debts were paid to his beloved wife Polly Tyler for the use of her family." James Beaseley, who died in 1829, gave some livestock to each of his two children and the remainder of his estates, valued at $1,011, to his "beloved wife Sarah." Lawrence Bradley, who died in 1819, allowed his widow, Betsy, to make an important decision: "I wish my wife at her own discretion to give what she thinks proper to my children as they come to age. . . ."

The remaining nine testators bequeathed the bulk of their estates to their wives until the widow remarried or the youngest child came of age. Eli Hillhouse, Polly's husband, was one of these. So was Patrick Money, who wrote his own will and stated his general intention in succinct, if unorthographic, prose. He gave "all my property that I possess unto my wife Elizabeth Money to have and to hold her life time unlest she shud git maried agine iff married again then I give ekewell share with the children of a state of dowr." In at least one case, the intent of a will was quickly frustrated. Nancy Fletcher was the executor of her husband John's estate, which was given to her during her widowhood. The will itself was dated December 2, 1825; by October of 1826, Nancy and her new husband were suing to obtain the one-third dower allowed by law.

Like most wills, those of Lawrence County tell us little about the romantic and emotional aspects of marriage. Phrases like "beloved wife" appear often, but they probably reflect literary conventions rather than the feelings of the individuals. Even the fact that men willed more property to their wives than was necessary may have resulted less from affection for them than for concern for the children. What is apparent, however, is that three-quarters of the Lawrence County husbands wanted their wives to take responsibility for the children and the family farm. Moreover, in the fifteen cases in which the testator named someone to execute his will, three men gave their wives sole authority and eight more made them co-executors. It would seem that the farmers of Lawrence County, and probably the farmers of Arkansas in general, believed that women could take on many responsibilities regarded elsewhere as masculine; indeed, these husbands apparently expected that their wives would take over for them when they were gone.[22]

The economic contributions of these Arkansas women were significant, but they were not unique. Women in all parts of the United States were involved in making a living for their families or themselves. Plantation mistresses and mid-Atlantic farm women toiled in the home, in the farmyard and garden, occasionally in the fields, and they sometimes managed agricultural operations.[23] Unmarried women and widows in Philadelphia actively controlled their own economic affairs,[24] and middle-class women in upstate New York and Petersberg, Virginia, made important contributions to the economic welfare of their families.[25] The combination of their high fertility and their function as "deputy husbands," however, make Arkansas women more traditional than these other groups. The conditions of the southern frontier stimulated Arkansas women to recreate a role that had worked in the past under similar circumstances.

~

But there was more to a woman's life than having children and working. According to a significant body of literature, middle-class and upper-class women in the Northeast were learning to marry for love, to limit the size of their families, and to devote a great deal of attention to the moral development of their children. They operated within "women's sphere," a separate realm from that of men, which freed women from the responsibility of outside employment and placed them in charge of affairs relating to family and home.[26] As the evidence of working women indicates, the spheres of men and women were less separate and less limiting than this model suggests.[27] Nonetheless, there was a body of prescriptive literature that defined proper behavior for ladies and taught them how to achieve it. Arkansas women were exposed to those ideas, as were women on other frontiers, and they put some of them into practice.[28]

The *Arkansas Gazette* apparently believed its readers were interested in proper feminine behavior since it reprinted pieces on the subject from eastern newspapers. One of these, "Whisper to a Wife," which appeared in March 1828, explained the ground rules of romantic marriage, emphasizing that the woman's role was to avoid conflict at all cost. Not long after, another borrowed piece advocated "simplicity of dress" for women. Not "gorgeous ornaments," but " a decent garb . . . concealing those beauties that would obtrusively force themselves upon our observation, . . . can render even beauty more amiable . . . and compel us to adore virtue thus personified in woman."[29]

The *Gazette* also provides evidence that some Arkansas women were admired for personifying "true womanhood." According to her obituary, published in February 1829, Mrs. Jane Woodward of Lafayette County suffered from the flu for twelve days, bearing her pain "with the fortitude of a christian and philosopher." She then died "perfectly composed and resigned, without a single murmur or struggle." When Mrs. Ester Harris of Batesville died a few months later, it was said that "society has lost one of its most useful ornaments." She too "died a christian," "seemed perfectly reconciled to her fate," and during three months of illness "was never heard to murmur." Hetty Bean, wife of Crawford County legislator Mark Bean, was given a lengthy obituary that dwelt on her role as a Christian and a member of the Methodist Episcopal Church. According to the author, in her final hours Hetty awoke several times to tell of dreams in which she met an angel.[30]

Hiram Whittington, who had first found the women of Little Rock extremely crude, later revised his opinion. Early in 1830 he began "to think some of our charming damsels quite interesting." He went riding with one and announced that the local "ladies are as good horsemen . . . as the men." He began to spend more time with women and developed a tolerance for the effects of the frontier on the opposite sex: "We have some beauties here, if they are raised in the woods." Even Rebecca Barkman had a young daughter of sixteen with "a mouth so sweet that one would almost forfeit heaven to kiss." The young miss Leana Barkman was to Whittington a "perfect child of nature, uncorrupted by the artificial polish of a heartless world." A polite society was emerging in the city, and the young bachelor found himself invited to a "tea-party, a candy pulling, an egg nog, [and] a wedding." Eventually the females became too sophisticated for Whittington's New England work ethic: "The women (or, I should say ladies, for they do not suffer you call them anything but ladies) get up in the morning, sometimes before breakfast, sometimes after, spend the forenoon in dressing and the afternoon in visiting."[31]

One of Little Rock's premier ladies was Mary Ashley, wife of Chester Ashley. Mary wrote to her son William, away at school in New York, about upcoming marriages in the Ashley circle, suggesting that "if the young people would only let me arrange such matters for them I think I could match them more suitable." She was also very mindful of her responsibility for the development of her children's character. Having William away at school "and so entirely committed to the charge of strangers" was "painful" and gave her "much anxiety and uneasiness." In her letters, she expressed her concern for him and gave him the advice she would have liked to give in person: "dear Will, you cannot imagine how anxious I am to have you loved and esteemed by your kind instructors . . . , I would much rather have you loved for your great qualities rather than admired for brilliant ones but I feel that my son might aspire to both . . . , I trust my dear boy will try and master his ugly passions and strive to gain the love and esteem of the good and estimable."

Mary's maternal sensibilities did not prevent her from offering William economic counseling that was grounded in Arkansas reality. While warning that he must pursue a profession before indulging his "present predilection for farming," she pointed out "our small farmers have to labour hard and live plain in order to make the ends of the year meet and I know it is hard for those accustomed to a different life to conform to such hardships."[32]

Nor were the Little Rock elite sheltered completely from the harsh realities and responsibilities of an agricultural society. Matilda Fulton, the wife of then secretary of the territory and later U.S. Senator from Arkansas William Fulton, spent a winter day in 1832 in a smokehouse, butchering nine hogs with the assistance of a slave. Two days later she gave birth to a child, assisted by four other Little Rock women, including the wife of Governor John Pope. Just as we may assume that butchering swine was a common enough activity among Arkansas women, so also was the gathering together in times of childbirth or illness or any other important event.[33]

~

Contemporaries painted the women settlers of Arkansas in the same colors they used for the men, making them seem rustic, crude, and generally unattractive. Again the portrait is not so much false as it is exaggerated. Other sources make clear that Arkansas women raised large families and exercised responsibilities that went beyond the household. This behavior placed them outside the norms of female behavior in the contemporary Northeast, and made them seem more like women who lived a century earlier. It also made them highly functional where they were. But this was no rebellion. The evidence suggests that Arkansas women were very interested in eastern styles and mores; the differences they manifested were accommodations to a frontier reality that would change over time. And that change would come in no small way as a result of the efforts of these women. When it asked Congress for a preemption law in 1829, the legislature of Arkansas Territory extolled the "bold and fearless" settlers: "Here they came where all was gloom, here they established their homes and here they are raising a hardy race of sons."[34] There is no reason to attack the unconscious chauvinism of the legislators, but it is important to recognize that just as sons included daughters so also the "bold and fearless" were women as well as men.

six

Inequality, Social Class, and Sectionalism

Economic inequality is a relative condition having to do with the difference between one person's income or wealth and that of someone else. For the student of society, past or present, inequality is a powerful tool, lending itself to measurement and to comparison. Recently, for example, Alice Hanson Jones measured the distribution of wealth among Americans in 1774 and demonstrated that it was similar to that found by a 1962 study of consumer units in the United States done by the Federal Reserve. Among the revolutionary generation, the richest 30 percent of the population owned 84 percent of the wealth—mainly slaves, real estate, agricultural equipment and crops, commercial inventories, and personal property; in 1962 the richest 30 percent of Americans owned 85 percent of all wealth, now consisting of bank balances, investments, houses, cars, and myriad other forms of assets. The pie had changed vastly over time, but the pieces were about the same relative size.[1]

Social class is a more difficult concept to define, and for many Americans, a difficult one to appreciate. The United States lacks a feudal tradition and has been characterized by the absence of social distinctions, at least among white people. Economic opportunity has also created at least the illusion of mobility. Alexis de Tocqueville, who believed that "the social state of the Americans is eminently democratic," stressed that his thesis was based on mobility rather than equality: "It is not that in the United States . . . there are no rich . . . but wealth circulates there with incredible rapidity, and experience shows that two successive generations seldom enjoy its favors."[2]

Still, historians have demonstrated the existence of class cleavages throughout the Jacksonian society that Tocqueville described.[3] In the South, slavery was permanent enough and racial prejudice intense enough that caste rather than class best describes the strata of black people. Historians have also found significant distinctions among whites, usually on the basis of whether or not they owned slaves. Early in the twentieth century, Ulrich B. Philips argued that the planters dominated not only the economy but also the politics and the society of the South. In the period after World War II, this concept was challenged by Frank Owsley, who argued that the planters were a small minority among slaveholders and a tiny minority among southern householders. For Owsley, it was the agricultural middle class of the South, the yeomen farmers or plain folk, as he called them, who were the economic and political strength of the region. In recent decades, a large and rich body of scholarship has grown up around the theme of antebellum class structure, providing us with a clearer view of southern society yet not defining classes in any precise way.[4]

~

What then was it like out in Arkansas, on the frontier of the slaveholding South? Was white society relatively equal or unequal with respect to wealth, and if unequal, were there significant strata that we might call classes? The distribution of wealth we can determine from the sample of 987 taxpayers in 1840. Their taxable property was assessed at what seems to have been market value. Land, for example, could have been purchased at less than the $5 per acre that was its average valuation, but since much taxable land was improved for agricultural purposes, the assessment was probably realistic. Similarly, $554 for a slave, $63 for a horse, and $13 for a head of cattle were all average values within the normal market range. Town lots, invested capital, and mills are more difficult to evaluate, but the revenue laws and the tax valuations suggest that assessors attempted to approximate real worth.

Per capita taxable wealth varied greatly between the lowlands and the highlands. For Arkansas as a whole it was $1,269, but in the lowlands it was $2,052, and in the highlands only $744. Median wealth tells us more about the average settler: it was $225 for all of Arkansas, $300 for the lowlands, and $190 for the highlands. The major portion of wealth, 72 percent for the state as a whole, was made up of land and slaves, and the great difference in regional wealth was the result of the heavy ownership of those items in the lowlands. Livestock constituted a larger proportion of the highland wealth than of the lowland wealth, but the average lowlander owned more of it.

The distribution of wealth in Arkansas in 1840 was markedly unequal. The wealthiest 10 percent of sample taxpayers throughout the state owned 70 percent of the taxable wealth. Inequality was significantly greater in the lowlands, where the richest 10 percent owned 72 percent of the wealth, than in the highlands, where the comparable figure was 61 percent.[5] Frontier Arkansas was apparently more unequal than were the colonies on the eve of the American Revolution or the South as a whole on the eve of the Civil War. Jones's study of 919 estates for 1774 produced a distribution of total personal wealth in which the top 10 percent owned 51 percent of total wealth. The property taxed by Arkansas was only about 85 percent of what Jones found on the inventories, however, and some of the remainder, in particular clothing, household utensils, and farm implements, was more widely distributed than most Arkansas taxable property. Gavin Wright's analysis of wealth in the South in 1860 indicates that the wealthiest southerners owned 62 percent of real estate and 59 percent of personal property.[6]

One factor that mitigated the disparity of wealth inequality in Arkansas was the availability of land without purchase. Only a third of taxpayers owned land, yet many of the landless were making use of it. Fifty-four percent of taxpayers owned no acres but did have livestock: these landless cattlemen owned 51 percent of the horses and 43 percent of the cattle in the territory. Thus their herds of livestock were nearly as large as those who did own land. Some of these landless taxpayers may have been recent immigrants who had not yet had time to purchase a tract; some may have been holding preemption rights for later use. In any event, they were using land for farming or grazing or both. Whether squatters or herdsmen, these taxpayers had a means of agricultural production and were less impoverished than the term nonlandowner suggests.

The structure of households in Arkansas provides another perspective on inequality. Of the 987 taxpayers, 412 can be identified in the census of 1840, and the distribution of wealth among these census households is significantly more equal than that among taxpayers as a whole. The richest 10 percent of households owned only 62 percent of the wealth instead of the 70 percent owned by the taxpayers (Table 10). The reason for the difference is that many young men with little property, some of them taxpayers only by virtue of the poll tax assessed on males 21 and above, lived in households headed by older and richer men, perhaps their fathers or brothers. There were about 565 males over 21 in these 412 households and 182 of them lived in households of which they were not the heads. Of these taxpaying, non–heads of household, 121 or 66 percent were in their twenties. Thus the wealth of 565 taxpayers was located in 412 households, subsuming younger taxpayers under older heads of households. Extrapolating from the sample of households, we may assume that our original 987 taxpayers lived in about 684 households that included 303 taxpaying males who were not the heads of their households and that most of these non–heads were young men in their twenties.

The distribution of wealth among households was more equal than among taxpayers because the non–heads of household had little property. Since most of them were young, it is possible, indeed likely, that they would become heads of household and acquire more wealth over time. The distribution of wealth among taxpayers was particularly unequal because Arkansas contained such a high proportion of young men, 6.7 percent more males in their twenties than the United States as a whole. Statistics aside, inequality was probably also eased by the structure of family and households that placed so many of those with little or no property in the homes of those who were more fortunate.

TABLE 10

Distribution of Taxable Wealth by Deciles, Taxpayers and Households

Deciles	Taxpayers			Households		
	N	Wealth	%	N	Wealth	%
Highest	98	879,744	70.2	41	342,406	61.8
Ninth	98	172,011	13.7	41	89,940	16.2
Eighth	98	85,566	6.8	41	46,672	8.4
Seventh	99	49,483	4.0	41	29,722	5.4
Sixth	99	28,270	2.3	41	18,741	3.4
Fifth	99	17,439	1.4	41	11,917	2.1
Fourth	99	11,007	0.9	41	7,654	1.4
Third	99	6,803	0.5	41	4,538	.8
Second	99	2,317	0.2	42	2,574	.5
Lowest	99	0	0.0	42	298	.0
Totals	987	1,252,640	100.0	412	554,462	100.0

Mitigated by several circumstances, the distribution of wealth in frontier Arkansas was still remarkably unequal, but was this inequality related to an important class structure among white Arkansans? Many would argue that the pattern of unequal wealth is simply evidence of a characteristic American social structure that might be called classless inequality. In this view, status in the United States is and has been largely a matter of wealth, and individuals have always had opportunity to acquire wealth and therefore to improve their status. Equality before the law and economic mobility have eliminated the circumstances that created social distinctions in Europe and allowed social classes only a vestigial existence in this country.[7] Before we discuss social classes in the South and investigate their existence in Arkansas, it is useful to consider the phenomenon generally.

Stanislaw Ossowski, a Polish sociologist, argues that the schemes of social stratification devised by social analysts of the past and present can be divided into three types: those that are based on a dichotomy, a twofold division of society; those based on gradation or ranking; and those based on economic functionalism.[8] The age-old tendency toward a dichotomous —us against them—view of society was expressed by Alexander Hamilton at the Constitution Convention of 1787 when he claimed that "in every community where industry is encouraged, there will be a division of it into the few & the many."[9] The idea of classes as gradations on a hierarchical scale is exemplified by Gregory King who placed the families of his own early modern England into twenty-six separate categories and by W. Lloyd Warner and his associates who divided American society of the 1940s into six classes, ranging from lower lower to upper upper and including the now commonplace designations of lower middle and upper middle.[10] James Madison argued for functional classes in Federalist No. 10 when he declared that "a landed interest, a manufacturing interest, a mercantile interest, a moneyed interest, with many lesser interests, grow up of necessity in civilized nations, and divide them into different classes, actuated by different sentiments and views."[11] But the most important functional system of classes, of course, was that of Karl Marx, which, of course, was based on the difference between those who owned the means of production and those who did not.

Ossowski's particular contribution is the insight that these disparate views of social class, both Marxian and non-Marxian, include three fundamental assumptions. There is implicit agreement that a class structure must be comprehensive in the sense of including all groups in society, that it must involve the distribution of significant privileges, and that the membership within a class must be relatively permanent.[12] Permanence is particularly important in an analysis of class structure in the United States. The unequal distribution of wealth has always been comprehensive, and it certainly involves important benefits, but are the unequal groups permanent, or does wealth circulate so rapidly that classes do not form? With that question in mind, let us turn back to the antebellum South.

Among modern southern historians who discuss social class, none is as forceful as Marxist Eugene Genovese, for whom the ownership of slaves is the basis for a dichotomous distinction. "The master class" is characterized by "an aristocratic, antibourgeois spirit with values and mores emphasizing family and status, a strong code of honor, and aspirations to luxury, ease, and accomplishment." The source of these values is the master-slave relationship. "The slave stood interposed between his master and the object his master desired . . . the slaveholder commanded the products of another's labor, but . . . was forced into dependence on the other." From this relationship the master obtained wealth, but it was also central to his "character making and myth making." Genovese's emphasis is on an elite, the planters, who were the true masters of southern society, yet the values and consciousness of this group apparently arose out of the experience of owning a slave. Thus, the most basic class distinction among southern whites was that between slaveholders and nonslaveholders.[13]

In contrast to Genovese, James Oakes writes about "master-class pluralism," arguing that there were significant differences among slaveholders and that many men moved into and out of the ranks of slaveholders. Yeomen farmers without slaves often acquired a slave or two. Small slaveholders, with one to five bondsmen, were less economically aggressive than middle-class slaveholders, who differed from the planters only in the degree to which they were successful. The master class was heterogeneous also in terms of its own makeup: it included immigrants, women, Indians, and free blacks. In all, estimates Oakes, the slaveholders included a third of all free households in the South down to 1850, after which the number of slaveholders decreased somewhat. Moreover, he believes that southern culture was shaped by history and the aspirations of all southerners; it was not dominated by the values of the slaveholder and the plantation. Not without meaning does Oakes entitle his book *The Ruling Race,* thereby emphasizing the dominant role of all whites. He does find important distinctions among southern whites, but that between slaveholder and nonslaveholder is merely one of a number of gradations, not a fundamental division.[14]

One way to test Oakes' theory and also to examine possible classes in Arkansas society is to divide Arkansas taxpayers into groups based on the ownership of slaves and other forms of property (Table 11). At the bottom of this hierarchy are the 127 propertyless taxpayers, perhaps two-thirds of whom, as we have seen, were young men in their twenties. A second group, which we shall call nonslaveholders, consists of 674 taxpayers who owned taxable wealth but not slaves. The mean taxable wealth of this group was $517, but nearly 60 percent of them (399 taxpayers) owned only livestock and had a mean taxable wealth of only $142. The third group consists of 142 small slaveholders owning 1 to 5 slaves. They have a mean taxable wealth of $2,660. Finally, there were 44 large slaveowners with more than 5 slaves, who had a mean wealth of $11,978. Among these 44 are 12 slaveholders who probably fit the conventional definition of planter by owning more than 20 slaves.[15]

TABLE II
Social Classes by Section

	Lowlands		Highlands		Total	
	N	%	N	%	N	%
Propertyless	73	18.4	54	9.1	127	12.9
Nonslaveholders	224	56.6	450	76.1	674	68.3
Small slaveholders	71	17.9	71	12.0	142	14.4
Large slaveholders	28	7.1	16	2.7	44	4.5
Totals	396	40.1	591	59.9	987	100.0

These distinctions are significant in terms of property ownership, economic functionalism, and the historical literature, but were they permanent, or even long lasting? To answer that question, an attempt was made to discover the status of each taxpayer 5 years later, in 1845. The lack of tax records for 8 counties meant that only 739 taxpayers were eligible for linkage between 1840 and 1845. Of that group only 216 or 29.2 percent were actually matched. Historians have often treated the inability to find a person at a later date as evidence of that person's downward mobility. Economic failure is seen as the cause of this "lack of persistence."[16] For a number of reasons, I think we should resist that interpretation here. Most important is the fact that only a third of the original taxpayers owned land and the landless were particularly susceptible to horizontal mobility—just plain moving on—which may or may not have been downward social mobility. Perhaps they drifted purposelessly, but they may also have found better land to squat on or to purchase in a nearby county. Secondly, Arkansas was in the midst of rapid population change. New immigrants helped to double the population in the decade of the 1840s while many erstwhile Arkansans were moving to Texas. New counties were created, meaning that some taxpayers were in different jurisdictions even though they stayed in the same place. The inability to find a person's name on two lists, which were often only marginally legible and produced five years apart, in the midst of this social flux ought not to prove very much.

The class structure of the matched group of taxpayers provides positive evidence that taxpayers with property persisted more than those who did not.[17] Propertyless taxpayers make up only 6.5 percent of this group, about half their size in the original group of 687 taxpayers; on the other hand, the other classes are about the same size. The matched group is a reasonable representation of Arkansas class structure as we have defined it. Social change for this group is a good indicator of social change for the taxpayers as a whole. The nature of that change is given in Table 12.

TABLE 12

Classes in 1845 by Classes in 1840

	Classes in 1840				
	Property-less	Nonslave-holders	Small Slave-holders	Large Slave-holders	Total
CLASSES IN 1845					
Propertyless	3	10	1	0	14
Nonslaveholders	11	129	8	3	151
Small Slaveholders	1	12	21	2	36
Large Slaveholders	1	1	3	10	15
Totals	16	152	33	15	216

The class structure we have reconstructed seems meaningful but fluid. The propertyless who did persist did rather well: 11 moved into the ranks of the nonslaveholders and 2 became slaveholders. Eighty-five percent of the nonslaveholders remained in their very broad classification, but 13 became slaveholders and 10 lost their property. Three small slaveholders became large slaveholders, but 9 of them lost their slaves, including 1 who lost all his property as well. Three of the large slaveholders also lost all their slaves. Remarkably, the structure was much the same in 1845 as it had been in 1840, but one-quarter of the taxpayers were in a different class.

The class mobility of Arkansas taxpayers is high when compared with that of the tobacco-growing regions of Kentucky and Tennessee between 1850 and 1860. Donald Schaefer's categories of yeomen, small slaveholders, and large slaveholders are the same as the categories used here except that this nonslaveholder category includes nonlandowners who have other forms of taxable property. Table 13 compares the class stability.[18]

TABLE 13

Mobility Comparison: Arkansas over Five Years and Western Tobacco Region over Ten years

	N	Stable	Upward	Downward
ARKANSAS, 1840–45				
Nonslaveholders	152	129	13	10
Small slaveholders	33	21	3	9
Large slaveholders	15	10	0	5
Totals	200	160	16	24
Percent	100	80	8	12
WESTERN TOBACCO REGION, 1850–60				
Yeomen (landowners)	87	70	13	4
Small slaveholders	50	24	11	15
Large slaveholders	34	29	0	5
Totals	171	123	24	24
Percent	100	72	14	14

Note: Downward mobility for nonslaveholders in Arkansas was into the category of propertyless taxpayer; for western tobacco region yeomen it was into the category of tenant. Neither study allows for upward mobility by large slaveholders.

Close to the same percentage of Arkansas taxpayers changed classes in five years as did Schaefer's farmers in ten years. If we include the large number of propertyless taxpayers who also moved up during the same period, it is clear that Arkansas was a highly mobile society between 1840 and 1845.

The evidence here supports James Oakes' view that slaveholding was a rather common phenomenon.[19] There were 48 slaveholders in 1840, 12 of whom dropped out, and 51 slaveholders in 1845, 15 of whom were new. A total of 63 taxpayers, 29 percent of the sample, owned slaves at one time or another between 1840 and 1845, 36 of them constantly and 27 part of the time. This in a society where slaves were only about 20 percent of the population.

But how important was the change? The Genovese perspective suggests that being a slaveholder was very different from being a nonslaveholder. Oakes, on the other hand, seems to think it was not. Support for Oakes' position comes from the work of historian John Solomon Otto, who has investigated the nature of slaveholding among the plainfolk of Yell County, Arkansas. In Otto's perspective, the yeomen slaveholders of Yell County were not much different from their nonslaveholding neighbors. Self-sufficiency was their immediate goal, and the market was a secondary consideration. They treated their slaves not unlike hired hands: master and slave often worked side by side and even hunted together.[20] These bondsmen were not sources of social and political power but rather of labor. Their loss would mean more work for the family but probably not less status.

Nonetheless, slave ownership was associated with political power. The standard definition of a southern planter is a slaveholder with 20 slaves, which would be the equivalent of about 12 taxable slaves. Among the 987 taxpayers in our 1840 sample, there were only 12 men in this category, a little more than 1 percent. Planters were much in evidence, however, at the convention that wrote a state constitution for Arkansas early in 1836. Of the 52 delegates, 37 can be found in the extant tax records of the period, and of those, 27 are slaveholders, 6 of them planters by the definition we have used.[21] On the basis of this information, it seems the planters, who were 1 percent of the population, may have been 16 percent of the framers of Arkansas's constitution, and that slaveholders in general, who constituted 19 percent of taxpayers, were 73 percent of the framers. Thus, the distinction between slaveholders and nonslaveholders is a significant one even though the boundary was often crossed in both directions. Slaveholders were more apt to wield power than nonslaveholders, as Genovese has argued.

Particularly significant is the number of slaveowners who represented the small farmers of the northwest. At least four of the Washington County delegation were slaveholders, including David Walker, who led the fight for white representation; Crawford County had two slaveholding delegates; Izard County had one; and Lorenzo Clarke of Johnson County was a planter with nineteen taxable slaves. Thus, the nonslaveholders of Arkansas were willing to provide a degree of deference to the slaveholders even when both were out of the plantation environment.

On the other hand, the nonslaveholders who helped to write the Arkansas constitution of 1836 included some whose property would qualify them as common men. Among them were Elijah Kelly of Pike County who was assessed in 1836 for three horses, five cattle, and a hundred acres of land; Abraham Whinery of Washington County who owned only forty acres, a horse, and two or three head of cattle; and G. L. Martin of Greene County who seems to have owned only a horse. If the ownership of slaves made it more likely that a man would exercise political power, having only a modest amount does not seem to have disqualified him from exercising political power.

∼

Both inequality and social stratification in Arkansas were conditioned by geography: the lowlands were characterized by slavery, cotton, taxable wealth, and an incipient planter class, while the highlands were dotted with small farms and filled with a large and mostly white population. The potential for sectional politics was there, but there was little evidence of it until the fall of 1835 when Arkansas prepared a state constitution in hopes of being admitted to the Union.

David Walker, a Whig leader from Fayetteville and territorial legislator from Washington County, was the Paul Revere of Arkansas sectionalism. His midnight ride came in the form of a circular letter to his constitutents published in the *Arkansas Gazette* early in November of 1835, and the part of the British was played by lowland politicians who, in Walker's view, were attempting to grab more than their share of representation at the constitutional convention. Reporting on activity in the legislature, Walker claimed that when the election of delegates to the constitutional convention was discussed, representatives of the "east and south" pointed out that their section had the most wealth and claimed it should receive "additional representation equal to three-fifths of their slave population." A debate ensued in which other lowland representatives asserted that "districts" should have representation "independent of population," while most of the legislators from the north and west claimed that "the only true basis of representation was the freemen of the country."[22]

The following week, a writer who signed himself Senex took issue with Walker but in so doing confirmed the existence of sectionalism. Accusing Walker of being a "disappointed individual" whose goal was "to excite discord and sectional jealousies," Senex went on to claim that the apportionment problem had been solved when "the grand divisions" of the country had been given equal representation. He defined these divisions exactly as had Walker: the north and west was one and the south and east was the other. Senex felt the people of the north and west would not be swayed by Walker's alarmism because they had as much representation as the south and east and were able to protect their own interests. Thus, if Senex was correct, not only had the territorial legislature defined two sections, but it had made equality between them a standard of fairness with respect to apportionment.[23]

Representation was also a bone of contention in the constitutional convention. After a lengthy struggle, sectional concerns were accommodated by apportioning the state senate by districts positioned in relationship to what the *Gazette* called "the *imaginery* [sic] *line* which some demagogues have attempted to draw through the Territory (or State that shortly is to be)." Eight senators would come from the northern and western side of the line, eight from the southeastern side, and one from a center district that included Pulaski County, with the capital city of Little Rock, and its neighbors Saline and White counties. If the line was imaginary, the division was very real. Table 14 shows the remarkable socioeconomic differences among the divisions.[24]

TABLE 14

Sectionalism and the Arkansas Senate in 1836

Sections	Free Population	Slave Population	Cotton (lb. per cap.)	Mean Taxpayer Wealth
North and West	22,713	2,958	11	$ 770
South and East	16,706	6,350	135	$2,084
Center	3,513	687	9	$1,559

Note: Senatorial districts are given in the constitution of 1836, and the sectional divisions are clear from the order in which the districts are listed—north and west, center, and south and east. Population figures are from the territorial census conducted in 1835; cotton and wealth information are from census and tax records for 1840.

Equal representation for the "grand divisions" of north and west and south and east balanced the greater free population of the one against the wealth of the other. The free population of the north and west was 36 percent greater than that of the south and east, although the large number of slaves in the south and east meant that the total population of the north and west was only 11 percent larger. Had the senators been apportioned on the basis of white population, the south and east would have had significantly fewer than the north and west. The principle of sectional equality, however, meant that the lowland planters would have as much power as the highland farmers despite their difference in numbers. Indeed, the planters probably did better than that. The center district would be dominated by Pulaski County, which was much more populous than its neighbors and very politically sophisticated. Pulaski County did not grow a lot of cotton, but it had a very significant slave population and a good deal of wealth, and it was tied into the economic and political system of the south and east.

For our purposes, however, it is less important to determine who won the fight over apportionment than to understand what it was all about. By the time Arkansas entered the Union, it had developed a sophisticated agricultural economy that was producing commodities and also generating economic inequality and at least the beginnings of a class structure. The pronounced geographical differences of Arkansas meant that wealth tended to cluster in the lowlands in the hands of planters or incipient planters. Senex declared that the concept of sectional equality meant that the north and west need not fear being dominated, but it was the south and east that raised the issue, and it was the lowlanders who were afraid of being dominated. The Arkansas senate, apportioned on the basis of carefully structured districts, was designed to protect the wealth of the most economically successful group in the territory.

~

At the end of the territorial period, the distribution of property in Arkansas was markedly unequal. Frontier equality was a myth. On the other hand, as Tocqueville and David Potter have argued, what Americans really wanted was opportunity. It was acceptable to have losers provided that there was the possibility of winning. Mobility in Arkansas seems high enough to validate the system for the white people who were its only players. There also seems to have been a class structure in Arkansas, with the ownership of slaves a major distinguishing characteristic. Owners of a few slaves, however, were probably not very different in lifestyle or status from their neighbors who owned none. And wealth mobility translated into class fluidity. The planters in Arkansas were powerful in 1840 but hardly dominant, probably because they were few in number. On the other hand, the apportionment struggle associated with the constitution of 1836 indicates that they were beginning to act together on a sectional basis to protect their economic interests. Over time the lowland elite would become more numerous and more powerful. The percentage of planters among slaveholders was 4.9 percent in 1840, 8.53 percent in 1850, and 11.87 in 1860.[25] In the last year, the power of slaveholders, and of planters in particular, would be great enough to carry Arkansas out of the Union.[26]

But the class structure that reached fruition on the eve of the Civil War was only blossoming in Arkansas Territory. Territorial society was unequal, but classes were neither well defined nor very permanent. Upward mobility was high and downward mobility was not infrequent. The territorial period, it would seem, was a time to scramble and get what one could, even at the risk of a fall.

seven

The "Teeming Possibilities" of Territorial Politics

Jacksonian Americans were strongly attracted to opportunity. Since they possessed a large degree of political equality and a strong sense of self-worth, they were ready to define themselves through upward economic mobility.[1] For that purpose, Arkansas Territory offered many advantages. Most important was fertile land, much of it suitable for cotton cultivation. In addition, the organization of Arkansas Territory also meant the creation of new political offices that carried both salaries and influence. These were highly attractive positions, particularly for men possessed of more talent than wealth. Citizens of the territory could also expect aid from the national government in acquiring land, in making their lives and property safe from outlaws and Indians, in improving transportation so that their crops could be sent to market, and in creating public institutions. These were the opportunities that politics offered, and Arkansans pursued them, always with vigor and occasionally with frenzy.

A small but highly visible minority of immigrants to Arkansas were driven by political ambition and the promise of rapid economic and social mobility that were associated with political success. Most of these were young men who had seen action and commanded soldiers in the War of 1812, were trained in the law, and had influential family and friends in Kentucky or Tennessee. In a more general sense, they were united by the possession of talent and the belief that Arkansas Territory could provide them with fame and fortune just as earlier frontiers had done for others before them. Their ambition led them into politics, where opportunity beckoned, and that same ambition created a political culture of intense individual and factional competition. It was American politics, but territorial opportunity and Jacksonian ambition made it personal and competitive, sometimes deadly so.

~

The mentality of the politically ambitious is no better illustrated than in a letter written in 1819 by Robert C. Henry, a lawyer living in Hopkinsville, Kentucky. For nine months, Henry had been working to secure a judgeship in newly-created Arkansas Territory. Two of the three judges there had resigned, and he anticipated an appointment and "emigration to a new country."

Encouraging his brother to come to Arkansas, Robert described his own vision of a *"new country"*: It was more than "unspoiled forests & uninhabited prairies. It ought to be a country where society was in its infancy, a rude & indigested mass, which the hand of genius & merit could shape to its own purposes. Where government was in its first grade, where offices were not filled—in short where all the teeming possibilities . . . were yet to be unravelled."

Henry was very clear about how he would take advantage of the "teeming possibilities." "Should I be favored with the appointment of judge, I shall have it greatly in my power to serve my friends. The judges are the legislature and we could do almost as we pleased. In fixing the seat of government we can have an eye to some desirable tract of country . . . All our family & friends could settle there, . . . and should thus acquire standing & consequence in the Country."[2]

Robert Henry did not receive the appointment he coveted and apparently gave up his dream. Others, however, fulfilled the territorial ambitions he articulated. In April of 1836, Ambrose H. Sevier, delegate to Congress from Arkansas Territory and soon to be senator from the state of Arkansas, wrote to President Andrew Jackson about federal appointments in Arkansas. Sevier's concern related to the fact that his cousin, James Sevier Conway, was about to give up his current position as surveyor general and run for governor of Arkansas. Sevier had originally suggested that Conway's cousin, Colonel Whorton Rector, presently agent for the Creek Indians, be appointed the new surveyor general, but now he was recommending that it be given instead to Judge Edward Cross, a political ally but not a relative. Rector's brother, Elias, was a federal marshal, and expected a reappointment when Arkansas became a state. Sevier worried that "the people of Arkansas will consider that there is too much monopoly in the offices of Arkansas by my relatives and intimate friends." Nonetheless, after recommending the substitution of Cross for Whorton Rector, he went on to request that his father-in-law, Judge Benjamin Johnson of the Superior Court, be appointed to the federal bench.[3]

Robert Henry's dream was Ambrose Sevier's reality. Sevier headed a political faction known as the Family or the Dynasty, which had exercised dominant influence in Arkansas for some time, and which was also the local branch of the Jacksonian Democratic Party. Achieving control of the territory had not been easy. The dominance of the Family came only after bitter and sometimes bloody struggles among rival would-be elites, all of whom possessed the same sort of territorial ambition as Henry.

The prototype for these men was Robert Crittenden, the first secretary of Arkansas Territory and the younger brother of U.S. Senator John J. Crittenden of Kentucky. Robert Crittenden had joined the army in 1814, when he was seventeen years old, and became a lieutenant the next year. He also served in the Seminole Wars. Crittenden arrived in Arkansas five months before the new governor did. During that period, he used his authority as acting governor to declare the territory to be in the second stage of government and to order elections for a legislature and for a territorial delegate to Congress. Most importantly, he made appointments to all the newly opened positions in the territorial government and in the counties.[4] It was an audacious performance and an effective one. Starting from this base and aided by the frequent absences of territorial governors, Crittenden wielded great influence in Arkansas affairs for more than a decade.

The role of territorial politics in the fulfillment of immigrant ambition can best be studied in the biennial elections for territorial delegate to the U.S. Congress. In addition to being the territory's highest elected official, the delegate was charged with the vital task of influencing federal policies in favor of Arkansas. It was an important and potentially powerful position. James Woodson Bates, a Virginian who had graduated from Princeton and whose brother, Frederick, the former land commissioner, was now secretary of the Missouri Territory, won the election for delegate in 1819 and was re-elected in 1821. In 1819 Bates' closest rival was Stephen F. Austin, a land speculator and prospective town developer perhaps best known at the time as the son of Moses Austin. The younger Austin, who apparently did not campaign, was remarkably popular in south Arkansas. Two years later, Bates' opponent was Matthew Lyon, the septuagenarian former New Hampshire Congressman and Republican editor who was jailed by the Federalists under the Sedition Act. Lyon lost by only sixty-one votes, probably because territorial citizens blamed Bates for the hated Choctaw Treaty. Lyon claimed that the votes were miscounted, but Acting Governor Robert Crittenden refused to allow him to examine the returns. Crittenden had been a law partner of Bates and had appointed him to the circuit court.[5]

If the secretary favored James Woodson Bates in 1821, he seems to have chosen another candidate by the election of 1823. Henry W. Conway, scion of an influential Tennessee family, a lieutenant in the War of 1812, and the receiver of public monies in the Arkansas Land District, declared himself a candidate for delegate. At that time, Conway indicated that Bates, who was in Washington, had told him privately that he would not be a candidate for re-election. Crittenden then convinced two other candidates to drop out, and Conway easily defeated Maj. William Bradford, commandant of the army post at Fort Smith. Meanwhile, Bates complained that Conway had exaggerated his own reluctance to run and resented the fact that he had been effectively taken out of the race. Bates ran against Conway in 1825, raising the question of nepotism in regard to surveying contracts that Conway had gotten from his uncle, William Rector, the surveyor general in St. Louis. Conway cited his accomplishments, in particular the forced cession by the Quapaw Indians of their considerable holdings in the territory. This time he won 80 percent of the vote.[6]

The sea change in territorial politics came in 1827 when Conway broke with Crittenden and ran with the support of his own faction, which included William Woodruff, editor of the *Arkansas Gazette*, and Chester Ashley, the rising attorney, land speculator, and political insider. Conway defeated his opponent, Robert Oden, a talented but irascible and erratic young lawyer from Kentucky, who got only 19 percent of the vote. During the campaign, however, Oden disclosed that Conway had used six hundred dollars of public money for his own expenses. Crittenden attested to the facts of the charge, which he had undoubtedly supplied to Oden. In the aftermath of this bitter campaign, Conway published a letter in the *Arkansas Gazette* claiming that Crittenden had lied in an effort to influence the election and that the secretary would "resort to any measure, however base and grovelling." Crittenden responded with a challenge, and the two men settled their differences in a duel.[7]

Because of a law against dueling in Arkansas, Conway and Crittenden met on the east side of the Mississippi River opposite the mouth of the White River about 8:30 in the morning on October 29, 1827. "The discharge from Mr. Crittenden's pistol took effect in Mr. Conway's right side, . . . that from Mr. Conway's, passed through the left lappel [sic] of Mr.

Crittenden's frock coat without doing him any personal injury."[8] Conway's attending physician pronounced his wound "severe but not dangerous," but the delegate died on November 9, presumably of infection. Conway had left letters with William Woodruff, editor of the *Arkansas Gazette*, suggesting that Crittenden had set out to kill him and that the duel was a result of that purpose rather than an ordinary affair of honor. Crittenden denied the charge, but the duel between the secretary and the delegate made factional politics in Arkansas Territory more intense and bitter just as it strengthened the territory's reputation as a shockingly uncivil place.

Conway's political successor was his cousin, Ambrose Hundley Sevier, who narrowly won a special election for delegate. Sevier had moved to Arkansas from Tennessee in 1820, when he was only nineteen years old. He later described himself as an orphan at that time, without either friends or family in Arkansas Territory. In a narrow sense this may have been true, but Ambrose carried the surname of his famous great-uncle, John Sevier, the Indian fighter and governor of Tennessee, and he was quickly joined in Arkansas by his cousins, the Conways and Rectors. A popular figure and an adroit politician, Sevier won four more elections for territorial delegate; during the last election he ran without opposition. Crittenden, on the other hand, went into decline after 1827. Newly elected President Andrew Jackson replaced both the governor and the secretary of Arkansas Territory in 1829, ignoring Crittenden, who had hoped to become governor and now found himself without any office. He continued to be a political force as the leader of an opposition faction, but won only 34 percent of the vote in a race against Sevier in 1833.[9]

Sevier's second and third elections provide an insight into the nature of factional politics. In the election of 1829 he defeated Richard Searcy of Batesville, and in 1831 he won against Benjamin Desha of Arkansas Post. In both campaigns Sevier ran on his record of accomplishment in Washington, citing passage of the donation law that provided 320 acres to landowners displaced by the Cherokee Treaty of 1828 and a variety of federal expenditures in the territory. His opponents accused him of being involved in unseemly land speculation and of favoring his friends with offices. National politics played only a small role—Desha, in fact, claimed to be a Jacksonian.[10] Sevier won 54 percent of the vote in 1829 and 55 percent in 1831, but that apparent stability of support masks significant geographical shifts. Against Searcy, who was from the northern part of the territory, Sevier received strong support from the southern, slave holding counties; against Desha from the south, he ran well in the northern counties where there were few slaves.[11]

Long after the events, William F. Pope, Governor John Pope's nephew, provided a perceptive analysis of territorial politics as he witnessed them in 1832. "There were no vital questions on national politics dividing the two parties. It was merely a scramble for control of Territorial affairs—the 'Outs against the Ins.'" Pope was right. There was a good deal of political discussion and controversy in the newspapers, but most of it revolved around personal issues of ability, character, and ethics. Incumbents emphasized their records in Washington and what their influence could do in the future, and that seems to have been important to the voters. Henry Conway increased his vote percentage from election to election, but his 80 percent majority did not transfer to Sevier, who took only 48 percent against two other candidates in the special election of 1828. Sevier became untouchable only once he demonstrated that he could obtain legislation favorable to Arkansas. This focus on individual leadership rather than on party program also led, as Pope remarked, to an emphasis on "personality and invective" in the newspapers that led to a number of "hostile encounters."[12]

Arkansas Territory was a dangerous place where southern concepts of honor were part of a casual attitude toward violence in general.[13] Formal duels were only the tip of a murderous iceberg, but they were the combat of choice for ambitious politicians whose pretensions included gentility. Robert Oden fought a duel with William O. Allen, a militia commander and territorial legislator, at Arkansas Post in 1820. The issue was personal and trifling—Oden was playing with Allen's cane, which contained a hidden spear point, and he refused to give it back when Allen demanded it—but Oden was seriously wounded and his opponent died. Four years later, Judge Andrew Scott of the Superior Court of the Territory killed his fellow jurist, John Selden, because, it was rumored, Selden insulted Scott's female partner while the three played whist. In preparation for his possible death, Scott wrote a letter to his wife that made the issue seem more serious, claiming that he was not "tired of living" but was willing to risk death rather than "life in *disgrace*" as a consequence of "a host of injuries & insults heaped upon me."[14]

Dueling assumed a more political character as political factionalism intensified. During the same campaign as the Conway-Crittenden duel, Ambrose Sevier challenged Thomas W. Newton, who had studied law under Crittenden and was his close associate. The basis of their conflict was Newton's authorship of a newspaper piece critical of Conway. When their initial shots missed, the principals were convinced by their seconds to give up the combat.[15] A few years later, William Fontaine Pope, a nephew of Governor John Pope and a hot-headed young man, even by

Arkansas's standards, fought two duels against his uncle's political enemies. In the second encounter he died at the hand of a talented young lawyer and writer, Charles F. M. Noland of Batesville.[16]

The election of 1833 between Sevier and Crittenden produced more challenges. Crittenden called out Thomas Eskridge, who declined on religious grounds; and William Cummins, a Crittenden man, challenged Sevier, who refused because of his public duties. Then there was the vendetta of Robert W. Johnson, later a U.S. Senator from Arkansas. During the campaign, William Cummins and Absalom Fowler, both Crittenden supporters, had participated in a campaign to bring about the impeachment of Judge Benjamin Johnson, Robert Johnson's father and Sevier's father-in-law. Sevier had the charges thrown out by the Senate, but the young Johnson demanded personal satisfaction. When he arrived home from Kentucky in August 1833, Johnson challenged Fowler and Cummins, but each refused. Johnson then attacked Cummins on the street with a walking cane. Later he posted handbills calling Fowler a coward, and the two men had an impromptu shoot-out in downtown Little Rock but were arrested before either was hurt.[17]

The prevalence of dueling in Arkansas politics indicates how the circumstances of the territory heightened elements of ambition and competition that were part of American and southern society. Personal honor was involved in the duel between Conway and Crittenden in 1827, but intertwined with that issue was the conflict of their separate ambitions. The rivalry between the delegate and the secretary was intense, and their anger was real and personal. Other political duels were based on far less provocation. The willingness to challenge and to accept a challenge was part of the process of self-definition by which men announced their social class and their political ambitions and maintained them. Dueling was illegal, but it was condoned by popular opinion. Crittenden's fortunes went down after he killed Conway, but they were already moving that way. Equally significant is the fact that even the opposition admired the secretary's "coolness" when he napped on the ground while waiting for the combat to begin. Dueling, of course, could also remove one's political rival, a thought that must have occurred to more than one challenger.[18]

~

The governors of territorial Arkansas were an important part of the political environment, but they did less to define it than the younger men who scrambled for lesser offices. The chief executives were not without ambition, but their aspirations involved promotion away from the territory rather than in the territory, presidential approval rather than popular acclaim. On the other hand, factional politics could not always be avoided, and it could be as dangerous for a governor as for anyone else.

James Miller, the first governor of Arkansas Territory, got the job because he was a hero of the War of 1812, accepted it because he needed the money, and went to the territory with seeming reluctance. He left his wife at home in New Hampshire, delayed his departure, traveled slowly, and only reached his post in December of 1819, six months after the creation of the territory. By that time, Secretary Crittenden had organized the government, made his appointments, and held elections for both houses of the legislature. Miller responded to this activity by raising a legal technicality. The organic law of Arkansas was based on the Missouri law of 1812, which specified that the upper house of the territory was to be appointed by the president of the United States out of nominees made by the lower house. Crittenden had held an election for the upper house, an action he justified on the basis of an amendment to the Missouri law that had been passed by Congress in 1816. The governor did not think that the amendment applied to Arkansas, but the territorial legislature supported Crittenden's interpretation, and so did U.S. Attorney General William Wirt. Eventually Congress passed an act legalizing actions of the legislature to remove all doubt.[19]

The dispute illustrates an important difference between Crittenden and Miller. The secretary believed in stretching the rules in the interest of pleasing the people and building personal power. Seven years later a newspaper polemicist quoted him as saying that the governor of a territory should "mould it to his plastic hand."[20] Governor Miller, on the other hand, was more interested in correct and responsible behavior, in doing his duty, and in winning the esteem of his superiors. He was capable enough and well-liked in Arkansas, but he made little attempt to build a base of power. Indeed, he spent remarkably little time in the territory, in part because of ill health. He visited his family in New Hampshire for nine months in 1821, and in June of 1823 he left Arkansas for good a year and a half before he resigned his office in December of 1824. Crittenden was acting governor much of the time, and it was the secretary rather than the governor who shaped territorial politics.[21]

George Izard, Miller's successor, was also disappointed with the office. A member of a wealthy and prominent South Carolina family and a former major general in the War of 1812, he had hoped for a diplomatic post. Unlike Miller, however, Izard was both a meticulous administrator and a tough-minded and adroit politician. Unhappy at not being appointed governor himself, Crittenden chose to be out of the territory when Izard arrived in Little Rock at the end of May 1825, leaving the new governor to orient himself. Upon his return, the secretary found himself sternly rebuked for what Izard believed were sloppy administrative practices, and the two remained at odds ever after. Izard did not isolate himself, however; he became friends with Henry Conway, Ambrose Sevier, and Chester Ashley and gave each of them the title of lieutenant colonel in the territorial militia. The following year Crittenden and Izard clashed again when the secretary wanted to go to Washington at a time when Izard would also be out of the territory.

The Izard-Crittenden feud forms a backdrop to the election of 1827 when Conway parted with Crittenden and then was mortally wounded by the secretary in the famous duel. Izard was publicly identified as Crittenden's enemy in the political warfare of the period, but the governor was out of town during the election and apparently took no part in the struggle. His support may have encouraged Conway and his friends to attack Crittenden, but they acted out of their own motives.[22]

John Pope, appointed governor in 1829 after Izard died in office, was a former U.S. Senator from Kentucky. He was John Quincy Adams' brother-in-law, but a strong hostility toward Henry Clay drove Pope into Jackson's camp, and he worked hard for Old Hickory in the election of 1828. Having hoped to be named attorney general, Pope, like his predecessors, came to Arkansas with some reluctance. He was a genial man, however, in his late fifties, and, unlike both Miller and Izard, was accustomed to the style of western politics that was practiced in Arkansas. For several years he seems to have been comfortable and successful in his position, although he created a mild stir by publicly stating that his relationship to the territory was similar to that of an overseer to a plantation.[23]

Pope's problems began in 1831 with a resurgence of power by Robert Crittenden. No longer secretary, Crittenden was still the leader of the opposition to the Sevier party. Sevier trounced Benjamin Desha for the position of delegate to Congress, but Crittenden's faction won a majority of the legislative positions within the territory. When the legislature met, it awarded the position of public printer to Charles Bertrand, editor of the *Arkansas Advocate*, instead of to William Woodruff of the *Arkansas Gazette*. The lawmakers then went on to dispose of ten sections of land granted by Congress to the territory to finance the construction of a capitol building, trading the land to Crittenden in return for his large and stately home, which was to serve as the capitol. The *Arkansas Gazette* believed that Crittenden's home was overvalued and unsuitable and called for a veto of the measure. Several days later, Pope did reject the bill.[24]

Pope's veto of the Ten Section Bill made him the center of controversy in Arkansas politics. He undertook to manage the sale of the land as well as the construction of the statehouse itself, earning far more money for the territory than Crittenden's home was worth and beginning the construction of a still more expensive architectural monument that still stands, known now as the Old State House. The *Advocate* relentlessly attacked the veto and Pope's performance in general, and when Crittenden ran against Sevier in 1833, he spent much of his time criticizing the governor, who was not even in the territory at the time.[25]

Pope also offended members of his own party. William Fulton, who had replaced Crittenden as secretary, became angry when the governor placed Chester Ashley in charge of the statehouse project during Pope's absence. Fulton announced to the general assembly and the public that the governor had exceeded his authority in spending money for the statehouse without legislative approval. Pope also quarreled with William Woodruff. The governor apparently wanted the *Arkansas Gazette* to defend him more vigorously, particularly when the *Advocate* charged that Pope had overpaid Woodruff for public business. The governor was also upset because Woodruff published Fulton's charges. Woodruff, in turn, became angry when Pope apparently helped a third printer, William Steele, to settle in Little Rock and then provided him, in the *Gazette*'s phrase, with a "good fat job" printing a digest of territorial laws.[26]

Governor Pope's increasingly difficult tenure came to an end early in 1835 when President Jackson replaced him with William Fulton, the former secretary who had been with Jackson in the Florida campaign and who, unlike Pope, had a history of unwavering loyalty to the president. Some months earlier, Pope had published a six-thousand-word apologia that shed light on the circumstances of his demise. The governor was candid about his political loyalties: "I have given all the offices and jobs to the friends of Col. Sevier ever since we have been identified in the party struggles of the country." He was hostile toward William Woodruff, "a little toad of an editor," but he professed friendship for Sevier, whom he called upon to disavow Woodruff's behavior. The governor was clear about the motives of his enemies: "This appetite for spoil and plunder is the main spring of the machinery that is working against me."[27]

Pope was probably right. Having defeated their rivals, the Sevier forces were fighting among themselves. Woodruff's animosity seems to have arisen out of the increasingly competitive printing environment and out of his feeling that party service was not being rewarded enough. More so than earlier governors, Fulton was a man on the make. He was capable and ambitious and, most important, well-connected at the national level of government. He was allied with the Sevier party in Arkansas, but his chief asset was the friendship of Andrew Jackson. His undermining of Pope was nicely timed and deftly executed. During his brief tenure as governor, Fulton's chief action was to oppose immediate statehood for Arkansas, an unpopular position that did not prevent him from becoming one of the first two U.S. Senators of the state of Arkansas.

~

Overshadowed by territorial delegates and by governors and diminished by its dependence, both statutory and self-imposed, on the national government, the legislature of Arkansas Territory played a limited role in public affairs. Nonetheless, the territorial lawmakers supported the political ambition of their leaders and helped to secure a significant amount of federal assistance that benefited Arkansas and widened the economic opportunity that it offered.

The creation of new counties was an important task of the legislature, and it used the opportunity to celebrate territorial leaders. Miller County, named for the governor who had only recently arrived, was created in 1820; Izard, Crittenden, Conway, and Sevier counties were formed in 1825 and Pope County in 1829; in 1833 Johnson County was created and named for Judge Benjamin Johnson, Sevier's uncle; that same year Scott County immortalized Andrew Scott, the leading jurist of the Crittenden faction; and in 1835, Searcy County was named for Sevier's opponent in 1829. The glorification of local leadership continued after statehood. In 1838 Desha County was named after another of Sevier's opponents; Fulton County was created in 1842, Ashley County in 1848, and Woodruff County in 1868.[28] The business of honoring politicians was remarkably thorough, either non-partisan, or, more likely, carefully balanced between the parties. James Woodson Bates did not have a county named for him, but that was probably because he was immortalized in 1824 when Poke Bayou became Batesville. Robert C. Oden would seem to have had as good a claim as Searcy or Desha, but his involvement in the 1827 campaign and the Crittenden-Conway duel may have made him anathema to the Sevier party.

Petitions to the national government, memorials as they were often called, were another important task of the legislature. Seeing themselves as "under the benign care of a powrfell [sic] and truly just republic," the lawmakers were not loathe to request aid from Washington while they waited for the time that Arkansas would "join in full communion the great American family."[29] As we have seen, Native Americans were an important topic in these requests, particularly during the 1820s when the white settlers of Arkansas were worried about the presence of Quapaws, Cherokees, and Choctaws within the territory. The legislature argued that the existence of the Indians inhibited the development of the territory as white people envisioned it. Over time, however, the Indians became a positive force in the sense that they were used to justify changes in the public land system that would be beneficial to white citizens.

When the revised Choctaw Treaty became final in 1825, the legislature asked for "some provision either in money or lands" for what it believed were three thousand Americans living west of the new line. In a petition to President John Quincy Adams, it asked that all Indians be moved west of white settlements. If the new Choctaw boundary were implemented, the legislators argued Arkansans would face four times their number in "Savages" located on all sides of the territory. Despite two military posts, they would be inadequately protected, and while the Osage and the Indians of Texas were causing trouble in the South, "our Women and Children might be scalped by the Choctaws, Cherokees and roving tribes from Missouri and White River." The legislators thought it particularly unfair that the endangered people included veterans of the War of 1812, who "defended the Eagles of their Country . . . yet have no desire to embroil their country in an other Indian War."[30]

The Cherokee Treaty of 1828, which provided a "donation" of 320 acres to the dispossessed settlers of Lovely County, stimulated a new set of requests from the importunate territorial lawmakers. Noting that the settlers of Miller County and Crawford County had arrived earlier and stayed longer than those in Lovely County, the assembly asked that the 320-acre donation be extended to the settlers south of Fort Smith who were displaced by the Choctaw Treaty. It also claimed that some settlers had lost their homes because of the first Cherokee Treaty back in 1817 and asked that these victims of "treaty making mania" also be given a donation of land.[31]

The 1829 legislature made a bolder departure, asking for a donation of 160 acres for each settler who would take up residence within 24 miles of the frontier. A dense population was necessary, it claimed, because of the Indians: "The bold and fearless savage knows no law, but that of force." Using the same justification, the legislators drew up another petition 11 days later that suggested giving 160 acres to immigrants arriving within the next 2 years.[32] Requests similar to these were sent again in 1831 and 1833. By then the alleged victims of the Cherokee Treaty of 1817 had become truly pathetic, pioneers "driven again into the forest, without food, and almost without raiment, the loss of their homes, and their stock, reduc[ing] them to a chilling poverty."[33]

Preemption was another important issue in Arkansas. The territorial assembly viewed the right to purchase public land that one had already improved as an important element of economic opportunity and as a means of giving settlers security against land speculators. It was also a reward for pioneers who suffered hardships extending the frontiers of the United States: "Here they came where all was gloom, here they established their homes and here they are rearing a hardy race of sons." In 1820 the legislature asked to have preemption extended to land south of the Arkansas River, and in 1823 and 1829 it memorialized Congress for a new law that would reward the efforts of all settlers. Even when Congress did pass a general preemption law in 1830, the territorial assembly was unsatisfied. Pointing out that many Arkansans were living on unsurveyed land and could not file claims within the one-year deadline, it called for a broader measure that would have no time limit.[34]

In addition to preemption, the assembly made many other requests dealing with public lands. In 1833, for example, it asked that the price of land be reduced, adding boldly that "throughout the West, there is growing a feeling of dislike to the Older States, founded principally upon the obstinacy displayed in keeping up the price of the Public Lands."[35] The legislators petitioned for improvements in the land system, particularly for the appointment of a resident surveyor general. They asked that the Winter claims be settled so as to encourage immigration in the Arkansas Post area, and they called for compensation for the unwitting purchasers of worthless titles to Bowie claims land. They also made numerous requests for grants of land to finance public buildings—a statehouse, a university, a penitentiary, county courthouses, and county jails.[36]

Transportation improvements also bulked large among the petitions of the territorial assembly. The major public works item of the 1820s was the so-called Military Road that ran from Memphis to Little Rock, which was requested in 1823 and funded by Congress in 1824. The project bogged down, quite literally, in the marshland of eastern Arkansas, and even after it was built, parts of it washed out in periods of high water. The nominally complete highway was described by an assembly memorial in 1831 as having been in a "delipedated [sic] situation" for more than two years. Congress appropriated more funds, however, and by the time of statehood the overland trip from Memphis to Little Rock was much improved.[37] Meanwhile, the assembly had become much more interested in transportation. Between 1829 and 1835, in individual petitions the assembly asked the federal government to provide funds for a network of roads that would link Helena, Batesville, and the mouth of the White River with the Memphis-to-Little Rock road and would connect Little Rock with Chicot County; Little

Rock with Hot Springs and Washington; Clark County with Chicot County; Clark County with Louisiana; Jackson in Lawrence County with Fayetteville in Washington County; Point Chicot with Paracliffe to the east; and Helena with Memphis.[38]

Nor was water transportation neglected. In 1833 the assembly gave its support to the continuing federal effort to remove the Red River Raft. It also petitioned for the removal of the snags and sawyers that obstructed navigation on the Arkansas, the White, the Ouachita, and the St. Francis rivers, as well as on Bayou Bartholomew. A more ambitious request called for the construction of a canal connecting Bayou Bartholomew with the Mississippi River.[39]

Finally, the territorial assembly was intrigued by the possibility of reclaiming portions of the Mississippi delta by building levees. It argued, for example, that the 11-mile embankment created by the proposed Bayou Bartholomew canal would prevent the annual flooding of 2 million acres that would become available for growing cotton. Similarly the legislators argued that 450 miles of levee on the Mississippi and Arkansas rivers from the Louisiana line to Pine Bluff would create a million and a half acres of new cotton land. The cost of this project was reckoned at $225,000 and the immediate benefits in terms of lands at $2,750,000.[40]

Justifying another such project that would have constructed a levee along the Arkansas side of the Mississippi above Memphis, the assembly stated what was undoubtedly its rationale for all the petitions: "To Arkansas the general government have indeed been extremely liberal, but from Arkansas the general government may hereafter reasonably expect more than millions for remuneration. Her minds [sic], her navigable streams, her rich and fertile regions and her mild and temperate climate all bespeak her future importance to the government and proclaim the grand stand she must eventually take as a member of the union."[41] To some degree that argument was accepted in Washington, and a great deal of federal legislation did benefit Arkansas Territory. With respect to transportation alone, Congress spent $666,000, including $267,000 on the Memphis-to-Little Rock Road and $216,000 on the removal of the Red River Raft.[42]

~

Ultimately, of course, the benefits of being a territory had to be weighed against the gains that would come with statehood. The first public discussion of that issue was initiated by the *Arkansas Advocate,* which was founded by its editor, Charles Bertrand, in March of 1830. Bertrand had been Woodruff's apprentice at the *Arkansas Gazette,* but he was also close to Crittenden, and very quickly the *Advocate* became the organ of the Crittenden party in the same way that the *Gazette* supported the Sevier forces.[43]

Encouraged by the increasing population of Arkansas that was in the process of being documented in the census of 1830, Bertrand embraced statehood in August of 1830 with the ardor of a romantic nationalist. It would provide, editorialized the *Advocate,* "the *power* of punishing delin- quents at *home* and *demanding* our *rights* abroad" and was the "only means of sundering our shackles and giving us the rights and rank to which we are entitled." He described the current situation as "Territorial vassalage," and encouraged his readers to "look forward to the day, at no distant period, when we shall rank high in the proud Confederacy."[44] "Aristides" supported the paper's position, suggesting that territorial status, in Pope's metaphor, left Arkansans as slaves on the plantation. Statehood for this writer meant "*independence.*" Moreover, he predicted it would lead to a 1,000 percent increase in population.[45] News that the Chickasaw Indians would be removed west led the *Advocate* to suggest that Washington and Crawford counties were again vulnerable to being given to the Indians, and that only by becoming a state could Arkansas protect against this threat.[46]

State-nationalism is a good name for the *Advocate's* position. The paper suggested that the aspirations of Arkansans could not be fulfilled within the limitations of territorial status. Statehood for Arkansas was therefore analogous to independence, a significant idea in the early nineteenth cen- tury, when nationalism was a fresh and powerful concept, when the United States was still a youthful nation, and when Latin America was newly independent. The *Advocate* put its opposition on the defensive.

The *Arkansas Gazette* did its best to rain on the *Advocate's* parade toward statehood. "Henry," who had been publishing a series of letters in that newspaper defending Governor Pope and Secretary Fulton against charges leveled by the *Advocate,* shifted his attention to the new issue. He pointed out that the federal government paid twenty thousand dollars in salaries for the governor, secretary, judges, and legislators of the territory. Statehood, he estimated, would immediately cost at least fifteen thousand dollars for a constitutional convention, ten thousand dollars to redeem territorial script, and twenty-six thousand dollars for public buildings. "Henry" believed that a year after statehood Arkansas would have forty- five thousand dollars in new debt and annual expenses of twenty-six thou- sand dollars. He believed that they were "poor," having as yet "little to export" and that new taxes would be a hardship. He was not "willing to see the last cow and calf or the last bed and blanket sold from the poor settlers of the country" to satisfy the ambitions of those who wanted statehood. "Henry" also ridiculed the "fanciful" views of "Aristides" about the benefits of statehood. He argued that "we can be as industrious in a Territory as a State." "Henry" would make progress in a sensible fashion: "Let us first procure a comfortable living for our families and prepare to take upon ourselves a state sovereignty."[47]

"Henry's" views were those of the Sevier party. Woodruff took on the *Advocate* himself in a brief editorial that pointed out that President Jackson was prevented by law from locating the Chickasaws within any existing territory. He added that talk of statehood was foolish until Arkansas gained the necessary population.[48] As he announced his candidacy for re-election in April of 1831, Ambrose Sevier addressed what he called the "excitable question" of statehood. He believed that Congress would require a territory to have about fifty thousand people before considering it for statehood, which meant that Arkansas had no immediate opportunity. Sounding very much like "Henry," Sevier was content with territorial status, "taxed high and deeply in debt, I believe we are pursuing our true interest by remaining as we are." "*In the absence of your instructions*," he would be "disposed to oppose" statehood until Arkansas was out of debt and had both the necessary population and "the means to support a State Government."[49]

Both sides in this early discussion of statehood accused each other of partisan political purposes, and surely both were right.[50] Having been removed as secretary by President Jackson, Crittenden probably believed that another territorial appointment was unlikely and that statehood offered him a better chance of winning a high office. On the other hand, the Sevier party was in control of the territory and not interested in immediate change. Both Desha in 1831 and Crittenden in 1833 took the position that statehood should immediately follow the achievement of the necessary population, but each also said he would do nothing without consulting his constituents.[51] On that basis, the issue was not important in either campaign.

Statehood did become an issue early in 1834 when Arkansans learned that Sevier, ignoring his earlier position, had requested that the House committee on territories examine the feasibility of Arkansas becoming a state. In a long address to his constituents, the delegate explained the extraordinary circumstances that prompted his action. Michigan was applying for admission. Since the Missouri Compromise of 1820, the entrance of a new free state was always balanced by the entrance of a new slave state to maintain the sectional balance in the Senate. If Arkansas did not act immediately, Florida might become the slave state to balance Michigan, and

Arkansas might have to wait a quarter of a century for Wisconsin to pursue statehood. Sevier believed "this not an unfavorable opportunity for our admission," Arkansas should be able to escape "trammels upon the subject of slavery," strike a good bargain with respect to its natural resources, and have Congress finish up the most important "works of internal improvements." Still, Sevier was still concerned about the population of Arkansas and its "embarrassed condition," apparently a reference to territorial finances. Were it not for Michigan, in his opinion, "it would be the wiser policy to defer our application for a few years yet to come."[52]

A second debate over statehood was foreshortened by the fact that the former opponents were now proponents. William Woodruff noted that Sevier had gone against his earlier pledge not to act without consulting the people but had done so in their interest and without binding them and for reasons that were "strong and cogent." The editor called for debate upon the issue.[53] "Seventy-Six" responded seven days later, sounding the same theme of state-nationalism that had characterized the *Advocate* a few years earlier. "The people are a sort of semi-slaves, without self-government. There is something humiliating and revolting to the pride and spirit of freemen to be ruled by officers sent from a distance. It is too much like the condition of the old British colonies." "Seventy-Six" also appealed to sectional interests. "The western States," presumably the southwestern states, called to Arkansas to support them against "other sections." Brushing aside the concern over "a little taxes," he urged Arkansas to "shoulder her political fire-lock and fight with her western friends." "Hickory" in the same issue sounded the theme of economic growth to be associated with statehood. "Escape from the fetters of childhood" would move Arkansas from "weakness to strength—from poverty to wealth—as she increases in population so will she increase in riches."[54]

Despite a growing consensus for statehood within Arkansas, the road in that direction was a rocky one. Jackson's enemies were worried that the new states would vote Democratic in 1836, and Congress authorized Arkansas and Michigan to conduct censuses to determine whether they could become states, but it refused to enable them to draw up constitutions. Eventually Michigan decided to write a constitution anyway and simply to request statehood, and Arkansas adopted the same strategy, except that Governor Fulton refused to go along until he had the support of President Jackson. Meanwhile, a census conducted in 1835 gave Arkansas a population of 52,240, more than was necessary for statehood. Sectionalism, as we have seen, emerged in October of 1835 as the Arkansas legislature debated the apportionment of representation in the constitutional convention and again over the same issue during the convention itself in January of 1836. The lowland, slaveholding south and east united against the highlands in the north and west, which had relatively few slaves and a larger white population. Eventually, however, a constitution was written and presented to Congress. After a long struggle, the Jacksonian Democrats in Washington succeeded in bringing Arkansas into the Union in June of 1836.[55]

For our purposes, the most important thing about statehood was why Arkansans wanted it. Most impressive throughout the debates was the nationalistic argument first made by the *Arkansas Advocate*. Territorial status was fettered, unequal, and even shameful, while statehood would mean freedom, equality, and pride. At first the *Arkansas Gazette* looked down on this emotionalism and emphasized the economic realities, but that seems to have been a holding action. When they decided it was time to act, Sevier and his friends stopped talking about taxes and made their own appeals to nationalism. One senses, however, that neither the politicians nor the press had to change a lot of minds; the voters were more interested in the political destiny of Arkansas than in the costs associated with it. A group of Jackson County petitioners for statehood made it plain that they had come "from old and organized states" and wanted to be once again "upon a footing of equality with our brethren from whom we have separated."[56] Statehood was simply another form of territorial ambition.

Epilogue

We leave Arkansas somewhat as we found it. In the sixteenth century the land of the present state was inhabited by people who clustered in towns, cultivated the soil, and hunted in the vast area that remained. At the end of the territorial period, most Arkansans were farmers who hunted largely for sport. They may have been more numerous than the natives of de Soto's time, but the decentralized fashion in which they lived meant that their society was probably more rural than that of the protohistoric Indians. The Arkansans of 1840 were more involved in a market economy, however, and, of course, they benefited from a variety of technological improvements unknown even to the Spanish three centuries earlier. Whether they experienced more happiness and fulfillment than the aborigines they replaced is impossible to say.

The similarities between the Indians of 1540 and the Arkansans of 1840 are real, but they suggest a continuity that did not exist. The native population of the sixteenth century declined rapidly after the de Soto expedition, and for several centuries Arkansas was relatively unpopulated. Neither France nor Spain ever brought many people to Arkansas, and it was not until the early nineteenth century that the resettlement of the area began in earnest. Thus the period between depopulation and repopulation was elongated by the time it took the expanding Anglo-American population to push across the Mississippi River. In Massachusetts, the Pilgrims met Squanto, whose people had lived at Plymouth and had died before the Europeans arrived; in Arkansas, the American settlers knew nothing about the protohistoric Indians who had cultivated the land before them. Not that it would have made any difference. As their attitudes toward the indigenous Quapaws and the transplanted tribes made clear, the new Arkansans of the territorial period were greedy for land, jealous of Indian claims, and lacking in both charity and sentimentality.

On the other hand, the American citizens who settled Arkansas Territory have often been maligned unfairly. They were little different from other Americans of their region and their time, and in many respects very similar to the ordinary run of southerner that Grady McWhiney calls "crackers." McWhiney, however, claims that crackers disliked work, placed a great deal of importance on leisure activities, and cared little about progress. Contemporary critics said the same thing about Arkansans, but we have seen that the allegation was exaggerated if not false. Some settlers moved to the territory to avoid the legalistic justice or the regimented work that was associated with older societies, but most came in the hope of improving themselves in an economic sense. Some of that sought-after improvement was simply improved subsistence brought about by available land, but there is also much evidence of market-oriented production and capitalist acquisition. On balance, it would seem that most territorial settlers were pushed west by their ambition rather than being lured to the frontier by a promise of freedom and ease. And if their houses, furnishings, food, and manners were rougher than those of the East, and if they took violent action against one another from time to time, it was not necessarily because roughness was a lifestyle they enjoyed or had inherited from Celtic ancestors as McWhiney suggests; rather, it may have been that making a place for oneself in a "new country" was a difficult and dirty job done under conditions that encouraged physical conflict.

By the end of the territorial period, the settlers of Arkansas had created an effective agricultural economy. They were producing significant amounts of cotton in the lowland areas where that was possible, growing corn everywhere, and raising large quantities of livestock. At the request of their territorial government, the United States had made important transportation improvements that would improve the marketing of commodities as well as making things easier for new immigrants. Economic opportunity existed and so did an infrastructure that would create still more. Over the next two decades, plantation agriculture became increasingly important, and cotton became the staple crop for which William Woodruff had hoped.

Arkansas Territory did offer the kind of economic abundance that David Potter believed was characteristic of the United States. Hunters lived as well as they wanted and enjoyed excellent sport. Farmers produced enough corn and livestock for a bountiful subsistence and probably sold some of their surplus. And cotton planters produced large and valuable crops on the bottomlands of the south and east. In addition, the newness of the territory provided several avenues of rapid upward mobility: the manipulation of Spanish Grants and other forms of land speculation attracted the energies of a small group of clever and avaricious men, and the existence of new political offices was similarly exciting to ambitious men with some claim to leadership ability. In general there seems to have been a large amount of economic mobility. The agricultural economy allowed people to improve their circumstances; other possibilities sometimes speeded the process, but occasionally there was downward mobility as well.

Indeed, the distribution of wealth in Arkansas was very unequal, and a large portion of the adult, male taxpayers owned little or no taxable wealth. Most of these men were attached to households where there was property, and many of them would acquire their own over time. Moreover, while land ownership was a minority phenomenon, land usage was widespread as settlers squatted on the public domain. White society in Arkansas was markedly unequal, but there seems to have been little grinding poverty—corn, livestock, and wild game were too available. Still, the concept of frontier equality is a myth. Inequality in Arkansas was on the same order as it was in the rest of Jacksonian society. But then Tocqueville was probably correct in asserting that Americans did not want equality but rather the opportunity to improve their own relative standing. That description seems to fit the settlers of Arkansas Territory, and, if true, it also means that they got what they wanted. In that sense, the settlement of Arkansas was very much a part of the American experience.

But if it was a national experience, the settling of Arkansas was also a southern phenomenon. Restless ambition was a characteristic of Jacksonian America, but only southerners dealt with the condition by carrying slaves to rich new soil located near rivers and by growing cotton that was carried by steamboats to New Orleans. And if slavery and cotton were characteristics of the South, so also were the hogs and corn that were raised all over Arkansas. In Arkansas as in the rest of the South, there was a social structure that was defined in part by the ownership of slaves. The distinction between slaveholder and nonslaveholder was not rigid; upward and downward mobility was common, and so was intermittent slaveholding. Social classes among the white settlers of Arkansas seem more like gradations than permanent categories. On the other hand, the promise of statehood galvanized the lowland planters into protecting their section against the more populous farm-dominated northwest. Fluid though it was, the planter class was both self-conscious and politically effective.

By the time of the Civil War, the Arkansas economy seems to have fulfilled the promises made for it by local boosters in the 1820s. The census of 1860 asked heads of households to estimate the value of their real and personal property. If this amount is added up for each state and divided by the total inhabitants, a figure for per capita wealth is obtained. This figure is hardly precise but provides a good estimate of the relative wealth of the thirty-four states. Arkansas ranks sixteenth, ahead of Tennessee, North Carolina, and fourteen states from the North. The South in general had a high per capita income because of its agricultural success and because its slaves were a valuable form of property. Indeed, if slaves are removed from the denominator, creating a figure for wealth per white capita, then the master class of the South was much richer. Per capita wealth for Arkansas was $504; wealth per white capita was $677.[1]

Secession, slavery, more than 600,000 men, and the economy of the South all died in the Civil War. By 1880 the income of the average south-erner was roughly half that of the average northerner, and it did not make much relative improvement until the twentieth century.[2] Arkansas lagged behind most of the South; as late as 1940, personal income per capita in Arkansas was only 43 percent of the national average. It climbed rapidly and rather steadily in the next three decades, reaching 73 percent in 1970. Since then there has been little gain in relation to the country: in 1988 Arkansas personal income was 74 percent of the national average, and the state ranked forty-seventh in that category.[3]

The image of Arkansas since Reconstruction has reflected the eco-nomic hard times and the backwoods lifestyle that lingered within the state. Opie Reed carried on the tradition of the Arkansas Traveler in a newspaper of that name that he founded in 1877, making fun of Arkansas backwardness. And in 1903 Thomas W. Jackson published a collection of similar humor called *On a Slow Train Through Arkansas*, the title of which became a metaphor for regional underdevelopment. Apparently no one had trouble getting the joke in 1945 when the *Reader's Digest* quoted a fictional notice on a bulletin board in a defense plant in the North: "One pair of shoes for sale. Owner returning to Arkansas." In these and other image-making pieces of popular culture, the Bear State image was updated and continued.[4]

Arkansas has made considerable economic progress since World War II, but it remains poor by national standards. Many Arkansans believe that their state has always been economically backward. The existence of this self-critical myth makes it easier for them to accept the hard economic realities that still exist and to make do with a smaller portion of opportunity and economic reward than most Americans. One can thank God for Mississippi, which traditionally was ranked fiftieth to Arkansas's forty-ninth in personal income, and perhaps now also for West Virginia and Utah, forty-ninth and forty-eighth in 1988 when Arkansas moved to forty-seventh, and accept the way things are because they have always been this way except when they were worse. But they have not always been this way.

The argument of this book is that men and women, black and white, created a successful economy in Arkansas when whites were masters and blacks were slaves; presumably they can do the same when both are free. Indeed, as we have seen, Arkansas has made much economic progress in recent decades. Another very encouraging development is the election of native Arkansan and long-time governor, Bill Clinton, to the highest office in the land. Clinton's success appears to be creating a new and positive image for Arkansas that will serve as an antidote to the persistent theme of backwardness. Thus, there is reason for optimisim that Arkansas will fulfill the ambitions of its modern citizens even better than it did those of its territorial settlers.

Appendix: Statistical Note

Microfilm copies of extant early Arkansas tax lists are available at the Arkansas History Commission. The 987 sample taxpayers in this set of data were drawn from the 10,000 or so names on assessment lists from the 25 out of 39 counties for which they were available. The randomness of the sample was insured by selecting a taxpayer by lot from among the first 9 on the first list and then each ninth taxpayer thereafter. Business partnerships, estates, and illegible cases were ignored, and the next ninth taxpayer was selected.

Lowland counties and the number of sample taxpayers are: Arkansas 25, Chicot 37, Desha 28, Jefferson 38, Lafayette 9, Mississippi 21, Monroe 16, Phillips 48, Pulaski 62, Randolph 36, Saline 35, and Union 41. Highland counties and the number of sample taxpayers are: Benton 34, Carroll 56, Conway 42, Crawford 72, Hot Spring 30, Independence 61, Johnson 51, Madison 47, Pike 14, Pope 47, Searcy 19, Washington 99, and White 19.

The household database was created by linking sample taxpayers with household heads in the manuscript version of the U.S. Census of 1840, which is available at the Arkansas History Commission. The 412 taxpayer households that resulted from this effort are a random sample of the households associated with the 10,000 taxpayers.

The mean of a random sample is the best estimate of the population mean, but its reliability depends on the size of the sample and the variation among the individual cases, both of which are taken into account by a statistic called the standard error. Estimates of population means are expressed in intervals around the sample mean that are associated with some stated degree of certainty. Table 15 below provides 95 percent confidence intervals to estimate population means for taxable wealth from 4 different sample groups.

Taxable wealth in this study consists of the assessed value of a taxpayer's acres of land, taxable slaves, taxable horses, taxable cattle, all of which were relatively widespread, and also of town lots, invested capital, and mills, which were owned by only a few taxpayers. Because wealth was unequally distributed, the confidence intervals in Table 15 are relatively large. We can, for example, be 95 percent confident only that the population of 10,000 taxpayers had a mean taxable wealth between $1,040 and $1,498, $229 below and above the sample mean of $1,269. The reader should note, however, that the lowest estimate for lowland wealth is $1,524 while the highest estimate for highland wealth is $873: we may be 95 percent confident that mean wealth for the population of taxpayers in the 2 regions was separated by at least $650. Probably the difference was much greater. The unequal distribution of wealth also means that the sample median is a better indicator of the average taxpayer's wealth than is the mean.

TABLE 15
Taxable Wealth Statistics and Estimates   (in dollars)

	Mean	Median	Standard Error	95% Interval (+ or -)
All taxpayers				
N=987	1,269	225	117	229
Lowland taxpayers				
N=396	2,052	300	269	528
Highland taxpayers				
N=591	744	190	66	199
Households				
N=412	1,346	346	163	320

Bibliographical Essay

All extant county records for early Arkansas are on microfilm at the Arkansas History Commission. For the early years of the territory, county tax records vary in the information they provide and are somewhat scarce. By 1840 they were uniform and sufficiently numerous so that it was possible to create a large and unbiased sample database. Arkansas County has a relatively complete run of tax records, which made it convenient for study. County records dealing with wills, probate materials, marriages, deeds, and other subjects are less numerous, but they do exist. The Lawrence County Probate Records were particularly useful to me.

Another important body of source materials is the land records located at the National Archives in Washington, D.C. Record Group 49, Private Land Claim Dockets—Arkansas consists of two boxes containing records relating to some 225 cases of disputed claims. Also in Record Group 49 is the correspondence between the General Land Office and its officials in Arkansas. Much of this is routine, and some of the more informative letters are published elsewhere, but it is a large and valuable collection.

Other manuscript collections dealing with Arkansas Territory are located at the Arkansas History Commission and in the Archives and Special Collections of the University of Arkansas at Little Rock. At the History Commission, I found the Chester Ashley Papers, the Potts Family Letters, and the Henry and Cunningham Papers particularly useful. Joseph Meetch's Diary is located at the Archives and Special Collections. I also used the separate collection of Chester Ashley Papers located there, the Martin Family Papers, Letter Book of the Arkansas Trading House, 1805–1810, and a number of small collections. I have also found some useful items in the Special Collections Division, University of Arkansas Libraries, Fayetteville, Arkansas, whose holdings concentrate on the period after 1840.

A large number of primary sources have been published. Chief among these are Clarence E. Carter's *Territorial Papers of the United States* (Washington, 1940–54), vols. 19–21, which cover Arkansas Territory. The *Arkansas Gazette* (1819–1991) contains much valuable information, as does the *Arkansas Advocate* (1830–36). Congress published many documents related to land in *American State Papers, 1789–1824* and *U.S. Congressional Serial Set, 1817–1827*. Morris S. Arnold and Dorothy Jones Core have published a most useful sourcebook on colonial Arkansas, *Arkansas Colonials, A Collection of French and Spanish Records Listing Early Europeans in the Arkansas, 1686–1804* (Gillett, Ark.: Grand Prairie Historical Society, n.d.).

Despite their biases, travelers' accounts are a very important source: these include Henry Rowe Schoolcraft, *Journal of a Tour into the Interior of Missouri and Arkansas* (London, 1821; reprint ed., Van Buren, Ark.: Argus Printers, 1955); Thomas Nuttall, *A Journal of Travels into the Arkansas Territory During the Year 1819*, ed. Savoie Lottinville (Norman: University of Oklahoma Press, 1980); George William Featherstonhaugh, *Excursion through the Slave States* (New York, 1844), and Friedrich Gerstäcker, *Wild Sports in the Far West*, intro. and notes by Edna L. Steeves and Harrison R. Steeves (1854; Durham, N.C.: Duke University Press, 1968). Hiram Whittington also provides an outsider's perspective in *Letters of Hiram Abiff Whittington, An Arkansas Pioneer from Massachusetts, 1827–1834*, ed. Margaret Smith Ross (Little Rock: Pulaski County Historical Society, 1956). William F. Pope, *Early Days in Arkansas* (Little Rock, 1895; reprint ed., Easley S.C., 1978) is an entertaining and seemingly reliable account of Arkansas affairs by a man who was something of a political insider.

Additional insight into the Arkansas Territory may be found in the enjoyable fiction of a territorial figure, Charles Fenton Mercer Noland, which is collected in Leonard Williams, ed., *Cavorting on the Devil's Fork, the Pete Whetstone Letters of C. F. M. Noland* (Memphis: Memphis State University Press, 1979). Gerstäcker also wrote a number of Arkansas stories that have been translated and published by James William Miller in *In the Arkansas Backwoods: Tales and Sketches by Friedrich Gerstäcker* (Columbia: University of Missouri Press, 1991).

Arkansas history before 1800 has benefited from much attention in the past decade. I have been most influenced by Dan F. and Phyllis A. Morse,

Archaeology of the Central Mississippi Valley (New York: Academic Press, 1983) and also "The Spanish Exploration of Arkansas," in *Columbian Consequences, vol. 2, Archaeological and Historical Perspectives on the Spanish Borderlands East* (Washington, D.C.: Smithsonian Institution Press, 1990). In addition to studies cited in the chapter notes, interested readers should consult three articles in the *Arkansas Historical Quarterly* 51 (Spring 1992): David Sloan, "The Expedition of Hernando De Soto: A Post-Mortem Report," 1–29; Michael P. Hoffman, " Protohistoric Tunican Indians in Arkansas," 30–53; and George Sabo III, "Rituals of Encounter: Interpreting Native American Views of European Explorers," 54–68. Morris S. Arnold has illuminated the French and Spanish period in two monographs: *Unequal Laws Unto A Savage Race: European Legal Traditions in Arkansas, 1686–1836* (Fayetteville, University of Arkansas Press, 1985) and *Colonial Arkansas, 1686–1804* (Fayetteville: University of Arkansas Press, 1991).

The best general study of Arkansas Territory is Waddy William Moore's unpublished dissertation, "Territorial Arkansas, 1819–1836," unpublished Ph.D. diss., University of North Carolina, 1962. Shorter but larger in perspective is the Arkansas chapter in Malcolm J. Rohrbough, *The Trans–Appalachian Frontier: People, Societies, and Institutions, 1775–1850* (New York: Oxford University Press, 1978). Politics has received more attention than other territorial topics. My account of events owes much to Lonnie White, *Politics on the Southwestern Frontier, 1819–1836* (Memphis, Tenn.: Memphis State University Press, 1964), which is detailed and accurate but lacks an interpretation. Margaret Ross, *Arkansas Gazette: The Early Years, 1819–1866* (Little Rock: Arkansas Gazette Foundation, 1969), is an excellent study that is broader than its title suggests. Native Americans are treated in David Baird, *The Quapaw Indians: A History of the Downstream People* (Norman: University of Oklahoma Press, 1980); Gilbert C. Din and Abraham P. Nasatir, *The Imperial Osages: Spanish-Indian Diplomacy in the Mississippi Valley* (Norman: University of Oklahoma Press, 1983); Arthur H. DeRosier, Jr., *The Removal of the Choctaw Indians* (New York: Harper & Row Publishers, 1972); and Robert Paul Markman, "The Arkansas Cherokees, 1817–1828," unpublished Ph.D. diss., University of Oklahoma, 1972. Orville Taylor, *Negro Slavery in Arkansas* (Durham: Duke University Press, 1958) is still useful. This relatively small group of monographs should be supplemented by a large and growing number of important articles in the *Arkansas Historical Quarterly*, many of which are cited in the chapter notes.

Books that have significantly affected my thinking about Arkansas Territory include David M. Potter, *People of Plenty: Economic Abundance and the American Character* (Chicago: University of Chicago Press, 1954); Francis Jennings, *The Invasion of America: Indians, Colonialism, and the Cant of Conquest* (Chapel Hill: Institute of Early American History and Culture, 1975); Grady McWhiney, *Cracker Culture: Celtic Ways in the Old South* (Tuscaloosa: University of Alabama Press, 1988); Sam Bowers Hilliard, *Hog Meat and Hoecake: Food Supply in the Old South* (Carbondale, Ill.: Southern Illinois University Press, 1972); *Laurel Thatcher Ulrich, Good Wives: Image and Reality in the Lives of Women in Northern New England, 1650–1750* (New York: Oxford University Press, 1983); *Alice Hanson Jones, Wealth of a National to Be: The American Colonies on the Eve of the Revolution* (New York: Columbia University Press, 1980); Stanislaw Ossowski, *Class Structure in the Social Consciousness* (New York: Free Press, 1963); Eugene D. Genovese, *The Political Economy of Slavery: Studies in the Economy and Society of the Slave South* (New York: Random House, 1965) and *The World the Slaveholders Made: Two Essays in Interpretation* (New York: Random House, 1969); and James Oakes *The Ruling Race: A History of American Slaveholders* (New York, Norton, 1982).

Articles that were particularly significant include C. Fred Williams, "The Bear State Image: Arkansas in the Nineteenth Century," *Arkansas Historical Quarterly* 39 (1980): 99–111; Daniel Scott Smith, "Family Limitation, Sexual Control, and Domestic Feminism in Victorian America," in Nancy F. Cott and Elizabeth H. Pleck, *A Heritage of Her Own: Toward a New Social History of American Women* (Simon and Schuster: New York, 1979), 222–45; Randolph B. Campbell, "Planters and Plain Folks: The Social Structure of the Antebellum South," in John B. Boles and Evelyn Thomas Nolen, eds., *Interpreting Southern History: Historiographical Essays in Honor of Sanford W. Higginbotham* (Baton Rouge: Louisiana State University Press, 1987); John Solomon Otto and Ben Wayne Banks, "The Banks Family of Yell County, Arkansas: A 'Plain Folk' Family of the Highlands South," *Arkansas Historical Quarterly* 46 (Summer 1982): 146–67; and Donald Schaefer, "Yeomen Farmers and Economic Democracy: A Study of Wealth and Economic Mobility in the Western Tobacco Region, 1850–1860," *Explorations in Economic History* 15 (1978): 421–37.

Notes

INTRODUCTION

1. Sarah Brown, "'The Arkansas Traveller': Southwest Humor on Canvas," *Arkansas Historical Quarterly* 46 (Winter 1987): 348–52, 356, 372–75.

2. Margaret Smith Ross, "Sandford C. Faulkner," *Arkansas Historical Quarterly* 14 (Winter 1955): 301–14.

3. *Letters of Hiram Abiff Whittington, An Arkansas Pioneer from Massachusetts, 1827–1834,* ed. Margaret Smith Ross (Little Rock: Pulaski County Historical Society, 1956), 17; G. W. Featherstonhaugh, *Excursion through the Slave States . . .* (New York, 1944), 95

4. Waddy Moore, "Some Aspects of Crime and Punishment on the Arkansas Frontier," *Arkansas Historical Quarterly* 23 (Spring 1963): 50–64.

5. Henry Ford White, "The Economic and Social Development of Arkansas Prior to 1836," (unpublished Ph.D. diss., Univ. of Texas, 1931), chap. 6; Waddy William Moore, "Territorial Arkansas, 1819–1836," unpublished Ph.D. diss., Univ. of North Carolina, 1962, chap. 7.

6. David Y. Thomas, *Arkansas and Its People: A History, 1541–1930* (New York: American Historical Society, 1930), vol. 1, 59–62; John Gould Fletcher, *Arkansas* (Chapel Hill: University of North Carolina Press, 1947), 108–09, 127–29; Harry S. Ashmore, *Arkansas: A History* (New York: W. W. Norton & Co., 1984), 52–53, 58–59; Morris S. Arnold, *Unequal Laws Unto a Savage Race: European Legal Traditions in Arkansas, 1686–1836* (Fayetteville: University of Arkansas Press, 1985), 183–93. A more realistic perspective is in David M. Tucker, *Arkansas: A People and Their Reputation* (Memphis: Memphis State University Press, 1985), 2–7.

7. James M. Woods, *Rebellion and Realignment: Arkansas's Road to Secession* (Fayetteville: University of Arkansas Press, 1987), 16, 29–30.

8. Malcolm J. Rohrbough, *The Trans–Appalachian Frontier: People, Societies, and Institutions, 1775–1850* (New York: Oxford University Press, 1978), 272–73, 281–82, 286–89.

9. David M. Potter, *People of Plenty: Economic Abundance and the American Character* (Chicago: University of Chicago Press, 1954), 84, 123, 155–56, 164–65.

10. Ibid., 90–93.

11. Robert H. Wiebe, *The Opening of American Society: From the Adoption of the Constitution to the Eve of Disunion* (New York: Vintage Books, 1984), 152. See also Randolph B. Campbell, "Planters and Plain Folks: The Social Structure of the Antebellum South," in John B. Boles and Evelyn Thomas Nolen, *Interpreting Southern History: Historiographical Essays in Honor of Sanford W. Higgenbotham* (Baton Rouge: Louisiana State University Press, 1987), 77; and Sean Wilentz, "On Class and Politics in Jacksonian America," *Reviews in American History* 10 (Dec. 1982): 58.

12. Joyce Appleby, "Commercial Farming and the 'Agrarian Myth' in the Early Republic," *Journal of American History* 68 (Mar. 1982): 849.

13. An illuminating discussion of this issue is in Allan Kulikoff, "The Transition to Capitalism in Rural America," *Journal of American History* 46 (Jan. 1989): 120–44. See also Charles Grier Sellers, *The Market Revolution: Jacksonian America, 1815–1846* (New York: Oxford University Press, 1991), 8–16.

14. Rowland Berthoff, *An Unsettled People: Social Order and Disorder in American History* (New York: Harper & Row, 1971), 177–84.

CHAPTER ONE

1. Henry Nash Smith, *Virgin Land: The American West as Symbol and Myth* (New York: Random House, 1950) is the classic study of this aspect of American culture.

2. Winthrop Jordan, *White Over Black, American Attitudes Toward the Negro, 1550–1812* (Chapel Hill: University of North Carolina Press, 1968), 90–91.

3. Francis Jennings, *The Invasion of America: Indians, Colonialism, and the Cant of Conquest* (Chapel Hill: Institute of Early American History and Culture, 1975), 15.

4. Russell Thornton, *American Indian Holocaust and Survival: A Population History Since 1492* (Norman: University of Oklahoma Press, 1987), chap. 2, esp. 25, 31. For a discussion and critique of estimates, see John D. Daniels, "The Indian Population of North America in 1492," *William and Mary Quarterly* 49 (Apr. 1992): 298–320.

5. Jennings, *Invasion of America*, 21–31. The growing literature on this subject includes Alfred W. Crosby, Jr., *The Columbian Exchange, Biological and Cultural Consequences of 1492* (Westport, Conn.: Greenwood Press, 1972), 35–63; William H. McNeill, *Plagues and Peoples* (Garden City, N.Y.: Doubleday, 1976), 182–91; Henry F. Dobyns, *Their Number Become Thinned: Native American Population Dynamics in Eastern North America* (Knoxville: University of Tennessee Press, 1983); and Alfred W. Crosby, *Ecological Imperialism: the Biological Expansion of Europe, 900–1900* (New York: Cambridge University Press, 1986).

6. Dan F. Morse and Phyllis A. Morse, "The Spanish Exploration of Arkansas," *Columbian Consequences, vol. 2, Archaeological and Historical Perspectives on the Spanish Borderlands East* (Washington: Smithsonian Institution Press, 1990), 198–99; Dobyns, *Their Number Become Thinned*, 41–42. See also Dan F. and Phyllis A. Morse, *Archaeology of the Central Mississippi Valley* (New York: Academic Press, 1983).

7. F. A. Kirkpatrick, *The Spanish Conquistadores* (Cleveland and New York: World Publishing Company, 1934), 154–66; John Bartlett Brebner, *The Explorers of North America, 1492–1806* (New York: World Publishing Company, 1933, 1964), 62–63; David B. Quinn, *North America from Earliest Discovery to First Settlements: The Norse Voyages to 1612* (New York: Harper and Row, 1977), 206.

8. John Swanton, *Final Report of the United States De Soto Expedition Commission* (Washington, D.C.: U.S. Government Printing Office, 1939); Dan F. and Phyllis A. Morse, "Spanish Exploration of Arkansas," Charles Hudson, "De Soto in Arkansas: A Brief Synopsis," *Arkansas Archeological Society Field Notes,* no. 205 (1985): 3–12. For a defense of the older view, see S. D. Dickinson, "The River of the Cayas, the Ouachita or the Arkansas River?" *Arkansas Archeological Society Field Notes,* no. 209 (1986): 5–11.

9. Edward G. Bourne, ed., *Narratives of Hernando de Soto,* 2 vols. (New York: Allerton Book Company, 1904; reprint ed., New York: AMS Press, 1973), vol. 1, vi–xvi, 113–14, vol. 2, 137.

10. Ibid., vol. 2, 123, 125.

11. Ibid., vol. 1, 123, 130, vol. 2, 31, 140.

12. Ibid., vol. 1, 123–24, 145, vol. 2, 147; Quinn, *North America,* 214–15.

13. Garcilaso de la Vega, *The Florida of the Inca,* trans. and ed. John Grier Varner and Jeannette Johnson Varner (Austin: University of Texas Press, 1951), 467–68.

14. C. Fred Williams et al., *A Documentary History of Arkansas* (Fayetteville: University of Arkansas Press, 1984), 8; David W. Baird, *The Quapaw Indians: A History of the Downstream People* (Norman: University of Oklahoma Press, 1980), 9–20, 23; Morse and Morse, *Archaeology,* 321; Marvin D. Jeter, "Tunicans West of the Mississippi: A Summary of Early Historic and Archaeological Evidence," in David H. Dye and Ronald C. Brister, eds., *The Protohistoric Period in the Mid-South: 1500–1700* (Jackson: Mississippi Department of Archives and History, 1986), 42–45.

15. Morse and Morse, *Archaeology,* 314–15; Crosby, *Ecological Imperialism,* 196–216; Dobyns, *Their Number Become Thinned,* 8–26.

16. Baird, *The Quapaw Indians,* 3–8; Morse and Morse, *Archaeology,* 321; Michael P. Hoffman, "Protohistory of the Lower and Central Arkansas River Valley in Arkansas," in Dye and Brister, *Protohistoric Period,* 30–34; Morse and Morse, "Spanish Exploration of Arkansas," 199, 204–05.

17. Baird, *Quapaw Indians,* 23, 27.

18. Brebner, *Explorers of North America,* 206–13, 245–55.

19. Morris S. Arnold, *Unequal Laws Unto a Savage Race: European Legal Traditions in Arkansas, 1686–1836* (Fayetteville: University of Arkansas Press, 1985), 5–6.

20. Henri Joutel, *A Journal of La Salle's Last Voyage,* intro. Darrett B. Rutman (New York: Corinth Books, 1962), 144.

21. Stanley Faye, "The Arkansas Post of Louisiana: French Domination." *Louisiana Historical Quarterly* 26 (1943): 636–39, 645–46.

22. Ibid., 652–54, 663–69; Arnold, *Unequal Laws,* 7–10. See also Morris S. Arnold, *Colonial Arkansas: A Social and Cultural History* (Fayetteville: University of Arkansas Press, 1991), 9–22.

23. Arnold, *Colonial Arkansas,* 31; Arnold, *Unequal Laws,* 16, 22.

24. Arnold, *Unequal Laws,* 33–34. For the various locations of the post, see ibid., 212–17.

25. Morris S. Arnold and Dorothy Jones Core, comps. and eds., *Arkansas Colonials: A Collection of French and Spanish Records Listing Early Europeans in the Arkansas 1686–1804* (Gillett, Ark.: Grand Prairie Historical Society, n.d.), 8–9, 14–15.

26. Capt. Philip Pittman, *The Present State of the European Settlement on the Mississippi,* intro. Robert R. Rea (1770; reprint ed., Gainesville: University of Florida Press, 1973), 40.

27. Baird, Quapaw, 26–34; Le Page Du Pratz, *The History of Louisiana,* ed. Joseph G. Tregle, Jr. (London, 1774; reprint ed., Baton Rouge: Louisiana State University Press, 1975), 318; Pittman, *Present State,* 40; Arnold and Core, *Arkansas Colonials,* 22.

28. Gilbert C. Din and Abraham P. Nasatir, *The Imperial Osages: Spanish–Indian Diplomacy in the Mississippi Valley* (Norman: University of Oklahoma Press, 1983), 115. Arnold, *Unequal Laws,* 84–87; Gilbert C. Din, "Arkansas Post in the American Revolution," *Arkansas Historical Quarterly* 40 (1981): 3–30.

29. Din and Nasatir, *Imperial Osages,* 5–23, 101.

30. Herbert Eugene Bolton, *Athanase de Mézières and the Louisiana–Texas Frontier, 1768–1780,* 2 vols. (Cleveland: Arthur H. Clark Company, 1914; reprint ed., New York: Kraus Reprint Co., 1970), vol. 1, 166–68; Arnold, *Unequal Laws,* 72–77; Din and Nasatir, *Imperial Osage,* 98, 100, 115, 122, 138, 193, 307.

31. Din and Nasatir, *Imperial Osages,* 56–57, 66–67, 110, 117, 213–14, 295.

32. Arnold and Core, *Arkansas Colonials,* 42–46.

33. Carl J. Ekberg, *Colonial Ste. Genevieve: An Adventure on the Mississippi Frontier,* 129–36; Pittman, *Present State,* 40.

34. *Colonial Arkansas,* 61.

35. Arnold and Core, *Arkansas Colonials,* 47–91; Arnold, *Unequal Laws,* 86, 90–91, 100. The value of agricultural production at Arkansas Post is figured from the table in Arnold, *Colonial Arkansas,* 62. Arnold's figure for average annual value is different from mine because there is an arithmetic error in his value for 1793.

36. John B. Treat to the Secretary of War, Nov. 15, 1805, Clarence Carter, ed., *Territorial Papers of the United States,* 26 vols. (Washington: Government Printing Office, 1934–69) vol. 13, 278–81. According to the French census of 1777, the total Quapaw population was 2.89 times the number of warriors, who were defined as males over twelve years. See *Arkansas Colonials,* 22.

37. Carter, *Territorial Papers,* vol. 13, 279–80.

CHAPTER TWO

1. U.S. Census Office, *Aggregate Amount of each Description of Persons Within the United States of America and the Territories in the Year 1810* (Reprint ed., Arno Press, 1976), 84; Arnold, *Unequal Laws,* 160–61. Margaret Ross is skeptical of the 1810 figures; see "The New Madrid Earthquake," *Arkansas Historical Quarterly* 27 (1968): 85.

2. "A Proclamation by Governor Clark," June 23, 1814, Carter, *Territorial Papers,* vol. 14, 789. Louis Houck, *A History of Missouri from the Earliest Explorations and Settlements until the Admission of the State into the Union,* 3 vols. (Chicago: R. R. Donnelley & Sons, 1908), vol. 3, 5. Houck transposes the 827 figure into 287, confusing his estimate of the Missouri population. The estimate of 1,588 persons in the total population is based on the ratio of free white males to the total population in 1810.

3. Walter E. McLeod, "Early Lawrence County History," *Arkansas Historical Quarterly* 3 (Spring 1944): 37–44.

4. Russell to Rector, Apr. 20, 1814, Carter, *Territorial Papers,* vol. 14, 756. See also the John C. Luttig letter from Pork [*sic*] Bayou dated April 16, 1815, Special Collections Division, University of Arkansas Libraries, Fayetteville, Arkansas.

5. Walter N. Vernon, "Beginnings of Methodism in Arkansas," *Arkansas Historical Quarterly* 31 (1972): 358–61.

6. McLeod, "Early Lawrence County," 41–42. Pulaski County settlers prior to 1814 are described in Margaret Smith Ross, "Squatters' Rights," *Pulaski County Historical Review* 4(2) (June 1956): 17–27; *Pulaski County Historical Review* 4(3) (Sept. 1956): 33–50; *Pulaski County Historical Review* 4 (3) (Dec. 1956): 51–66. Carter, *Territorial Papers,* vol. 15, 181.

7. Arnold, *Unequal Laws,* 136–39, 149–50, 155–65, 173–74. See also Houck, *History of Missouri,* vol. 2, 355–63, 376–79, 400–01; vol. 3, 1–9

8. Dallas T. Herndon, *Centennial History of Arkansas* (1922; reprint ed., Easley, S.C.), vol. 1, 142–43.

9. *Census for 1820* (Washington, 1821; reprint ed., New York, 1976).

10. Lonnie J. White, *Politics on the Southwestern Frontier: Arkansas Territory, 1819–1836* (Memphis: Memphis State University Press, 1964), 6–16.

11. The movement of the capital and the administration of public lands are discussed in chap. four; on steamboats, see Moore, "Territorial Arkansas," 151–67; see also Edwin C. Bearss and Arrell M. Gibson, *Fort Smith: Little Gibraltar on the Arkansas* (Norman: University of Oklahoma Press, 2d ed., 1979) and Margaret Ross, *Arkansas Gazette: The Early Years, 1819–1866* (Little Rock: Arkansas Gazette Foundation, 1969).

12. *Arkansas Gazette,* Dec. 27, 1825; "Memorial to Congress, Oct. 17, 1821," Carter, *Territorial Papers,* vol. 19, 148; Baird, *Quapaw Indians,* 51, 56–57, 61–70.

13. Din and Nasatir, *Imperial Osages,* 371–82.

14. Robert Paul Markman, "The Arkansas Cherokees, 1817–1828," (unpublished Ph.D. diss., University of Oklahoma, 1972), 74, 82–87.

15. Markman, "Arkansas Cherokees," 107; Ina Gabler, "Lovely's Purchase and Lovely County," *Arkansas Historical Quarterly* 19 (Spring 1960): 31–39.

16. *Arkansas Gazette,* Nov. 20, 1819.

17. "Memorial to Congress," Oct. 18, 1823, Carter, *Territorial Papers,* vol. 19: 557–58; "Memorial to Secretary of War," Oct. 18, 1823, *Territorial Papers,* vol. 19, 602–03.

18. Moore, "Arkansas Territory," 144–45.

19. Arthur H. DeRosier, Jr., *The Removal of the Choctaw Indians* (New York: Harper & Row Publishers, 1972), 58–59, 63–67, 169.

20. *Arkansas Gazette,* Oct. 7, Dec. 16, 1820. See also ibid., Jan. 20, 27, Feb. 3, and Feb. 17, 1821.

21. *Arkansas Gazette,* Apr. 7, 1821; ibid., May 12, 1821, ibid., Mar. 5, 1822; ibid., Mar. 29, 1825; DeRosier, *Removal of the Chocktaw,* 70–82; W. David Baird, "Arkansas's Choctaw Boundary: A Study of Justice Delayed," *Arkansas Historical Quarterly* 28 (1969): 205–08.

22. *Abstract of the Returns of the Fifth Census* (Washington: Duff Green, 1832; reprint ed., New York, Arno Press, Inc., 1976), 42; Gabler, "Lovely's Purchase and Lovely County," 34–39.

23. Robert Walz, "Migration into Arkansas, 1834–1880," unpublished Ph.D. diss., University of Texas, 1966, 57; Jack E. Eblen, "An Analysis of Nineteenth–Century Frontier Populations," *Demography* 2 (1965): 412. Sixth Census, *Aggregate Amount of Each Description of Persons* (Washington, D.C., 1841), 432–34; James E. Davis, *Frontier America: 1800–1840, A Comparative Demographic Analysis of the Frontier Process* (Glendale, Calif.: The Arthur H. Clark Company, 1977), 103–17.

24. *Sixth Census*, 432–34.

25. E. E. Dale, "Arkansas: The Myth and the State," *Arkansas Historical Quarterly* 12 (Spring 1953): 19–22; Dwight Pitcaithley, "Settlement of the Arkansas Ozarks: The Buffalo River Valley, *Arkansas Historical Quarterly* 37 (Autumn 1978): 203–22.

26. Moore, "Territorial Arkansas," 151–67; see also Walter Moffatt, "Transportation in Arkansas, 1819–1840," *Arkansas Historical Quarterly* 15 (Autumn 1956): 187–201.

27. *Arkansas Advocate*, May 12, 1830.

28. C. Fred Williams, "The Bear State Image: Arkansas in the Nineteenth Century," *Arkansas Historical Quarterly* 39 (Summer 1980): 99–105. See also Robert B. Cochran, "'Low, Degrading Scoundrels': George W. Featherstonhaugh's Contribution to the Bad Name of Arkansas," *Arkansas Historical Quarterly* 48 (Spring 1989): 3–16; and Leonard Williams, ed. *Cavorting on the Devil's Fork, The Pete Whetstone Letters of C. F. M. Noland* (Memphis: Memphis State University Press, 1979).

29. Richard C. Bremer, "Henry Rowe Schoolcraft: Explorer in the Mississippi Valley, 1818–1832," *Wisconsin Magazine of History* 66 (1982): 40–42.

30. Henry Rowe Schoolcraft, *Journal of a Tour into the Interior of Missouri and Arkansas* (London, 1821; reprint ed., Van Buren, Ark.: Argus Printers, 1955), 68–71.

31. Ibid., 80–81, 86–87, 155.

32. Ibid., 154, 156.

33. Ibid., 103–04; Yasukichi Yasuba, *Birth Rates of the White Population of the United States, 1800–1860: An Economic Study* (Baltimore, 1962), 62.

34. Bremer, "Schoolcraft," 46, 48.

35. George E. Lankford, "'Beyond the Pale,': Frontier Folk in the Southern Ozarks," in Robert J. Smith and Jerry Stannard, eds., *The Folk: Identity, Landscapes and Lores,* University of Kansas Publications in Anthropology, No. 17 (Lawrence: University of Kansas, 1989), 66.

36. Ted R. Worley, ed., "Letters From an Early Settler," *Arkansas Historical Quarterly* 11 (1952): 327–29; Vernon, "Beginnings," 358–59, 364; Ted R. Worley, ed., "Story of an Early Settlement in Central Arkansas," *Arkansas Historical Quarterly* 10 (1951): 125–28.

37. Musick and Parker to Clark, Aug. 1, 1816, Carter, *Territorial Papers*, vol. 15, 181.

38. Thomas Nuttall, *A Journal of Travels into the Arkansas Territory During the Year 1819,* ed. Savoie Lottinville (Norman: University of Oklahoma Press, 1980), ix–xx.

39. Ibid., 84, 102–03, 112, 127, 130, 132, 243.

40. Ibid., 85, 88–89, 112, 130.

41. Joseph Meetch, Diary of Travels in Arkansas, 1826–27, University of Arkansas at Little Rock Archives, h.4, b.3, f.87.2.

42. G. W. Featherstonhaugh, *Excursion through the Slave States . . .* (New York, 1944), 81, 84–86, 92.

43. Ibid., 87–90, 97, 135–36.

44. Ibid., 119.

45. Ibid., 131, 133, 135.

46. James William Miller, ed. and trans., *In the Arkansas Backwoods, Tales and Sketches by Friedrich Gerstäcker* (Columbia: University of Missouri Press, 1991), pp. 12, 21–22.

47. Friedrich Gerstäcker, *Wild Sports in the Far West,* intro. and notes by Edna L. Steeves and Harrison R. Steeves (1854; Durham, N.C.: Duke University Press, 1968), x, 157, 161.

48. Grady McWhiney, *Cracker Culture: Celtic Ways in the Old South* (Tuscaloosa: University of Alabama Press, 1988), xiii–xv, xxxviii–xli, 8.

49. Ibid., 24–25, 28, 38–50, 72–76, 81–83, 105–07, 128–30, 148–49, 229–37.

50. Ibid., 12.

51. James L. Skinner III, ed., *The Autobiography of Henry Merrill: Industrial Missionary to the South* (Athens: University of Georgia Press, 1991), 249, 259.

CHAPTER THREE

1. *Arkansas Gazette*, Nov. 18, 1820.

2. For additional agricultural boosterism, see *Arkansas Gazette,* "A Citizen," Nov. 20, 1819; Nov. 18, 1820; Nov. 9, 1824; Jan. 5, 1825; and "Franklin," Jan. 12, 1831.

3. Ibid., Feb. 4, 1823.

4. Ibid., Feb. 26, 1822; Apr. 16, 1822; May 17, 1825; Oct. 11, 1825; Dec. 13, 1825; Dec. 27, 1825.

5. Ibid., July 2, 1822; Sept. 23, 1823; June 28, 1825; Oct. 4, 1825; Oct. 11, 1825; Feb. 2, 1830.

6. See, for example, *Arkansas Gazette,* June 8, 1824; Aug. 18, 1825; Apr. 9, 1828; May 13, 1829.

7. Ibid., Sept. 14, 1824; Aug. 13, 1828; Sept. 13, 1831.

8. Ibid., Jan. 12, 1831.

9. The laws dealing with taxation are summarized under "revenue" in J. Steele and J. M. Campbell, *Laws of the Arkansas Territory* (Little Rock, 1835) and William MckBall and Sam C. Roane, *Revised Statutes of the State of Arkansas* (Boston, 1838).

10. See Appendix.

11. Patricia Cline Cohen, *A Calculating People: The Spread of Numeracy in Early America* (Chicago: University of Chicago Press, 1982), 191–204; Carroll D. Wright and William C. Hunt, *The History and Growth of the United States Census* (Washington: Government Printing Office, 1900), 38. See also Margo J. Anderson, *The American Census: A Social History* (New Haven: Yale University Press, 1988).

12. *Historical Statistics of the United States, Colonial Times to the Present* (Washington, D.C., 1975).

13. See Appendix.

14. *Compendium of the . . . Sixth Census* (Washington, 1941; reprint ed., Arno Press, New York, 1976).

15. Lewis Cecil Gray, *History of Agriculture in the Southern United States to 1860* (Gloucester, Mass.: Peter Smith, 1958) vol. 2, 709, 1027.

16. Alfred Dupuy, Lawrence County Loose Probate Records, Arkansas History Commission.

17. Sam Bowers Hilliard, *Hog Meat and Hoecake: Food Supply in the Old South* (Carbondale, Ill.: Southern Illinois University Press, 1972), 158.

18. Frank Lawrence Owsley, *Plain Folk of the Old South* (Baton Rouge: Louisiana State University Press, 1949), 24–25, 30–31, 34–36, 48–51; Forrest McDonald and Grady McWhiney, "The Antebellum Southern Herdsman: A Reinterpretation," *Journal of Southern History* 41 (May 1975): 155–57; Hilliard, *Hog Meat and Hoecake*, 122–24. For a negative view of plantation livestock, see Eugene D. Genovese, *The Political Economy of Slavery: Studies in the Economy and Society of the Slave South* (New York: Vintage Books, 1967), 106–18. See also McWhiney, *Cracker Culture*, chap. 3.

19. Hilliard, *Hogmeat and Hoecake*, 128–40; *Arkansas Gazette,* July 3, 1833; ibid., Sept. 2, 1834.

20. *Hilliard, Hogmeat and Hoecake,* 260 n. 34.

21. For example, the estate of William Mask, inventoried in 1833, had four hogs that were valued at fourteen dollars, see William Mask, Lawrence County Loose Probate Records.

22. *Arkansas Gazette*, Aug. 7, 1833; ibid., Aug. 5, 1834.

23. Except where otherwise noted, the analysis of Arkansas County here is drawn from S. Charles Bolton, "Inequality on the Southern Frontier: Arkansas County in the Arkansas Territory" *Arkansas Historical Quarterly* 41 (Spring 1982): 51–66.

24. Nuttall, *Journal*, 83; *Arkansas Gazette*, Dec. 13, 1825; ibid., Aug. 26, 1828; William F. Pope, *Early Days in Arkansas* (Little Rock: Frederick W. Allsopp, 1895), 65, 67.

25. Surprisingly little has been written about early Washington County or Fayetteville. A useful introduction is contained in the journal of the Washington County Historical Society, see Jerry E. Hilliard, "The Political-Social Elite in a Frontier Territorial Town: Fayetteville, Arkansas," *Flashback* 33 (1983): 18–21. Insight into patterns of trade in western Arkansas may be obtained from the Henry and Cunningham Papers in the Clara Bertha Eno Collection at the Arkansas History Commission. Both the census of 1840 and the tax records provide data on capital invested in merchandise. The figures vary widely, but it is clear that Pulaski, Crawford, and Washington are the top counties.

26. The taxpayers were traced by Meg Kilgore, who had no knowledge of the author's hypothesis.

27. Dewey A. Stokes, Jr., "Public Affairs in Arkansas, 1836–1850," (unpublished Ph.D. diss., University of Texas, 1966), 195.

28. Kirkbride Potts to Ann Potts, July 1830, Potts Family Letters, 1823–52, Arkansas History Commission, Small Manuscripts, Box LXIII, no. 19. A more general and lyrical statement of how a "poor man" could become successful in Arkansas agriculture is contained in Albert Pike's "Letters from Arkansas," *The New England Magazine* (Oct. 1835), available at Special Collections Department, University of Arkansas Libraries, Fayetteville, Arkansas.

CHAPTER FOUR

1. *Arkansas Advocate* (Little Rock, 1830–36), Jan. 12, 1831.

2. Jackson Payson Treat, *The National Land System, 1785–1820* (New York, 1910), 35–38, 85–86, 90, 94–97.

3. Malcolm J. Rohrbough, *The Land Office Business: The Settlement and Administration of American Public Lands, 1787–1837* (New York: Oxford University Press, 1979), 15–16, 92–96, 103–06.

4. Treat, *National Land System*, 175, 189; *Arkansas Gazette*, Sept. 23, 1820. Copies of the official maps designating the land districts are at the University of Arkansas at Little Rock Archives and Special Collections.

5. Boswell to Meigs, May 9, 1820, Record Group 49, Letters from Registers and Receivers, General Land Office, National Archives, Batesville, vol. 9; Dec. 20, 1840; ibid., Fayetteville, Box 5; ibid., Miller to Waywood, Feb. 2, 1834; ibid., Washington, Box 6; Extracts from Boswell to Meigs, Oct. 22, 1821, and Boswell and Trimble to Meigs, Jan. 12, 1822, Regarding the Nomination of William Rector, 17th Congress, Record Group 46, National Archives, Sen 17B–A3 (2), National Archives. Copies of the last were provided to me by Frances Ross.

6. For annual land sales, see *American State Papers, Legislative and Executive of the United States in Relation to Public Lands* (Washington: Duff Green, 1834), 7:531–32; preemption sales are collected in Henry Ford White, "The Economic and Social Development of Arkansas Prior to 1836," (unpublished Ph.D. diss., University of Texas, 1931), 202.

7. Rohrbaugh, *Land Office Business*, 137–40; Smith to Graham, Oct. 31, 1823. Letters from Registers and Receivers, Little Rock, vol. 10; Boswell to Graham, September 10, 1825, ibid., Batesville, vol. 9; Noland to Graham, Dec. 25, 1826, ibid., Batesville, vol. 9.

8. William Thomas Farnan, "Land Claims Problems and the Federal Land System in the Louisiana–Missouri Territory," (unpublished Ph.D. diss., Saint Louis University, 1971), 10, 28–29, 68, 149–50.

9. *American State Papers, . . . Lands*, vol. 2, 723–24, 727; ibid., vol. 3, 343–44, 355–57.

10. Record Group No. 49, Private Land Claim Dockets—Arkansas, National Archives, no. 75.

11. Farnan, "Land Claims Problems," 77.

12. Deed from McKenny to Russell, Nov. 15, 1813, Private Land Claim Dockets—Arkansas, no. 140; ibid., no. 85; Deed from Duvall to Russell, July 30, 1819, ibid., no. 60.

13. Carter, *Territorial Papers*, vol. 19, 631–32.

14. William D. Ferguson to Elijah Hayward, Apr. 23, 1834, Private Land Claim Dockets–Arkansas, no. 91 (John Grace).

15. *American State Papers*, vol. 2, 632–33; Heirs of Elisha Winter, H. Rept. No. 405, 22d Cong. 1st Sess., 226.

16. H. Rept. No. 303, 23d Cong. 1st Sess., 261.

17. Treat, *National Land System*, 246–49; Rohrbough, *Land Office Business*, 82–83, 87–88.

18. *Arkansas Gazette*, Oct. 7, 1823.

19. Ibid., Nov. 11, 1823.

20. Ibid.

21. Ibid., Apr. 20, 1824.

22. Ibid., Nov. 9, 1824.

23. The 1825 Tax Assessment for Arkansas County is available on microfilm at the Arkansas History Commission in Little Rock.

24. Treat, *National Land System*, 303–5; Hempstead to William Rector, Feb. 8, 1819, Private Land Claims Dockets—Arkansas, no. 1.

25. The best account of the entire episode is in Margaret Ross, *Arkansas Gazette: The Early Years, 1819–1866* (Little Rock: Arkansas Gazette Foundation, 1969), 35–39, 41.

26. Lonnie J. White, *Politics on the Southwestern Frontier: Arkansas Territory, 1819–1836* (Memphis: Memphis State University Press, 1964), 30–31.

27. Pulaski County Deed Records, 1819–1823, B, 12–15, Arkansas History Commission, Little Rock.

28. Ibid., 24–26, 28–29.

29. Ibid., 18–21.

30. *Russell v. Wheeler*, Hemp. 3 (Super. Ct. of Ark. Terr., 1821).

31. William Russell to Isaac Watkins, Jan. 22, 1822, Knight Collection; Arkansas History Commission; Pulaski County Deed Records, 1819–1823, B, 119–43.

32. White, *Politics*, 36.

33. *Arkansas Gazette*, June 11, 1828.

34. H. Doc. No. 114, "Instructions to Land Officers in Arkansas, &c," 20th Cong. 2d Sess., 2–7.

35. *Arkansas Gazette*, May 27, 1829.

36. White, *Politics*, 94–95; Carter, *Territorial Papers*, vol. 21, 356.

37. *Arkansas Gazette*, Feb. 10, 1829.

38. Ibid., Apr. 24, 1827.

39. H. Rept. No. 80, 21st Cong. 1 Sess., 3–7.

40. Preston to Graham, Oct. 10, 1829, S. Doc. No. 1, 21st Cong. 1st Sess., 321–28.

41. Private Land Claim Dockets—Arkansas, no. 14.

42. H. Rept. No. 80, 21st Cong. 1st Sess., 7–19.

43. George P. Kelley, "John J. Bowie, 1787–1859," *Phillips County Historical Quarterly* 12 (1974): 5–13; *Arkansas Gazette*, Feb. 9, 1831; *Sampeyreac and Stewart v. United States*, 7 Peters 459 (1833); Court Record relating to Arkansas Land Claims, 1824–32, National Archives, Record Group 49, Division D, Private Land Claims Division, Item 8.

44. See n. 47 below.

45. *Arkansas Gazette*, Jan. 26, Feb. 9, 1830.

46. H. Rept. No. 80, 21st Cong. 1st Sess., 8–11.

47. Acting Governor Fulton to the President, Aug. 3, 1831, Carter, *Territorial Papers*, vol. 21, 358–59; Cleland District, St. Augustine, Florida, Locations under Arkansas Court, Act of 1824, vol. 125, Private Land Claims, Item 9. Congressional action on behalf of Bowie claim purchasers took place in 1842 and 1849.

48. *Arkansas Gazette*, Sept. 4, 1844; Ashley Papers, Box 2, File 13, University of Arkansas at Little Rock Archives.

49. Rohrbough, *Land Office Business*, 203–05; *Arkansas Gazette*, Feb. 19, 1820, June 15, 1830, May 25, 1831, June 1, 1831.

50. Rohrbaugh, *Land Office Business*, 221–49. Data on land sales in Arkansas is from S. Ex. Doc. no. 41, 30th Cong. 1st. Sess., 166–81.

51. White, "Economic and Social Development of Arkansas," 190–93; *Arkansas Gazette*, Oct. 31, 1834.

52. *Arkansas Gazette*, Dec. 2, 23, 1834; ibid. May 12, Nov. 17, 1835.

53. Featherstonhaugh, *Excursion*, 119, 121–22; *Arkansas Gazette*, Sept. 1, 1835.

54. *Arkansas Gazette*, Mar. 1, 1836.

CHAPTER FIVE

1. Schoolcraft, *Journal*, 71, 86.

2. C. Fred Williams, et al., eds., *A Documentary History of Arkansas* (Fayetteville, Ark.: University of Arkansas Press, 1984), 16–17; Carl J. Ekberg, *Colonial Ste. Genevieve: An Adventure on the Mississippi Frontier* (Gerald, Mo.: The Patrice Press, 1985), 329.

3. *Letters of Hiram Abiff Whittington: An Arkansas Pioneer from Massachusetts, 1827–1834*, ed. Margaret Ross Smith (Little Rock, Pulaski County Historical Society, 1956), 1–2.

4. Ibid., 3–5, 10, 20; Newberry Farrar, "Jacob Barkman," *Arkansas Historical Quarterly* 19 (Winter 1960): 316–17.

5. *Arkansas Gazette*, July 22, 1829.

6. Featherstonhaugh, *Excursion*, 84–86, 114.

7. Ibid., 107, 113, 117–18; Friedrich Gerstäcker, *Wild Sports in the Far West* (Durham, N.C.: Duke University Press, 1968), 85–86.

8. McWhiney says little about women, but he provides many examples of criticism directed toward food, housekeeping, accommodations, and other things that involve women. See *Cracker Culture*, 81–85, 93–94, 117–18, 123, 126, 128, 130, 229–230, 234–38.

9. Daniel Scott Smith, "Family Limitation, Sexual Control, and Domestic Feminism in Victorian America," in Nancy F. Cott and Elizabeth H. Pleck, *A Heritage of Her Own: Toward a New Social History of American Women* (Simon and Schuster: New York, 1979), 226–36.

10. Yasukichi Yasuba, *Birth Rates of the White Population of the United States, 1800–1860: An Economic Study* (Johns Hopkins University Press: Baltimore, 1962), 61–63.

11. Not until after 1840 do Arkansas marriage records routinely give the age of the bride and groom. We do, however, have that data for 32 of 55 marriages performed in Independence County in 1839 and 1840. Eight of the 32 brides were 15 to 17 years and 11 were 18 to 20 years. See Independence County Records, Marriage Book, "A–B," 1826–61, Arkansas History Commission.

12. Yasuba, *Birth Rates*, 61–63.

13. Jack E. Eblen, "An Analysis of Nineteenth–Century Frontier Populations," *Demography* 2 (1965): 412–13; Richard A. Easterlin, "Factors in the Decline of Farm Family Fertility in the United States," *Journal of American History* 43 (Dec. 1976): 609–14; James E. Davis, *Frontier America, 1800–1840: A Comparative Analysis of the Settlement Process* (Glendale, Calif.: The Arthur H. Clark Company, 1977), 79–81.

14. Davis, *Frontier America*, 81–82.

15. Laurel Thatcher Ulrich, *Good Wives: Image and Reality in the Lives of Women in Northern New England, 1650–1750* (New York: Oxford University Press, 1983), 35–38, 49–50.

16. Taxpayers with clearly feminine names are 1.7 percent of the sample and households with no males over twenty are also 1.7 percent. Both of these criteria probably understate the number of female heads.

17. Smith to Hayward, Feb 11, 1832, Letters Received from Registrars and Receivers of Land, Arkansas, Little Rock, Box 5; Hayward to Registrar and Receiver in Fayetteville, March 18, 1834, Letters Sent to Registrar and Receiver, Vol. 4, 149; *Arkansas Gazette*, Dec. 22, 1835.

18. Eli and Polly Hillhouse, Lawrence County Loose Probate Records, Arkansas History Commission, Little Rock.

19. Andrew Criswell, Lawrence County Loose Probate Records.

20. The wills are those of James Beasley (1829), James Bellah (1827), Isaac Booth (1837), Lawrence Bradley (1819), John Bridges (1836), James Campbell (1835), John Coffelt (1836), George W. Cooper (1835), Reuben Corzine (1836), Thomas Delany (1817), John G. Fletcher (1825), Eli Hillhouse (1820), John Hobbs (1836), Ezekiel Hudson (1837), John H. King (1837), John McCarroll (1834), Robert McWilliams (1833) (filed under Robert M. Williams), Gasper Mansker (1831), David Marshall (1836), Patrick Money (1819), John Pierce (1833), John Tyler (1823), Peter Tyler (1832), and Henderson White (1835).

21. J. Steele and J. M'Campbell, *Laws of the Arkansas Territory* (Little Rock, 1835), 210–17.

22. For a similar interpretation of colonial wills, see Lois Green Carr and Lorena S. Walsh, "The Planter's Wife: The Experience of White Women in Seventeenth-Century Maryland," in Michael Gordon, ed., *American Family in Social-Historical Perspective,* 2d ed. (St. Martin's Press: New York, 1978), 270–72; contemporary urban wills are discussed in Suzanne Lebsock, *The Free Women of Petersberg: Status and Culture in a Southern Town* (New York: W. W. Norton & Company, Inc., 1984), 35–48.

23. Catherine Clinton, *The Plantation Mistress: Woman's World in the Old South* (New York: Pantheon Books, 1982), 16–35; Joan M. Jensen, *Loosening the Bonds, Mid–Atlantic Farm Women, 1750–1850* (New Haven: Yale University Press, 1986), 36–39.

24. Claudia Goldin, "The Economic Status of Women in the Early Republic: Quantitative Evidence," *Journal of Interdisciplinary History* 16 (1968): 375–404.

25. Mary P. Ryan, *Cradle of the Middle Class: The Family in Oneida County, New York, 1790–1865* (Cambridge: Cambridge University Press, 1981), 26–27, 201–04; Lebsock, *Free Women of Petersberg*, 148–53.

26. Gerda Lerner, "The Lady and the Mill Girl: Changes in the Status of Women in the Age of Jackson," in Cott and Pleck, *A Heritage of Her Own*, 182–96; Barbara Welter, "The Cult of True Womanhood: 1820–1860," in Michael Gordon, ed., *The American Family*, 313–33; Nancy F. Cott, *The Bonds of Womanhood: "Woman's Sphere" in New England, 1780–1835* (Yale University Press: New Haven, 1977), 23–26, 58–62, 64–74, 84–87; Carl N. Degler, *At Odds: Women and the Family in American from the Revolution to the Present* (Oxford University Press: New York, 1980), 8–20, 211–13.

27. Linda K. Kerber, "Separate Spheres, Female Worlds, Woman's Place: The Rhetoric of Women's History," *Journal of American History* 75 (1988): 9–39; Laura McCall, 'The Reign of Brute Force is now Over': A Content Analysis of Godey's Lady's Book, 1830–1860," *Journal of the Early Republic* 9 (1989): 218–36.

28. Julie Roy Jeffrey, *Frontier Women: the Trans-Mississippi West, 1840–1880* (New York: Hill and Wang, 1979), 4–10.

29. *Arkansas Gazette*, Mar. 12, 1828, and Jan. 27, 1829.

30. Ibid., Feb. 10, 1829, and Sept. 23, 1829.

31. *Letters of Whittington*, 15, 16, 18, 20, 25.

32. April 22, 1837, Oct. 18, 1840, and June 15, 1841, Chester Ashley Papers, Arkansas History Commission.

33. Conevery A. Bolton, "'A Sister's Consolations': Women, Health, and Community in Early Arkansas, 1810–1860," *Arkansas Historical Quarterly* 50 (Autumn 1991): 271–91, esp. 289.

34. Carter, *Territorial Papers*, vol. 21, 93–94.

CHAPTER SIX

1. Alice Hanson Jones, *Wealth of a Nation to Be: The American Colonies on the Eve of the Revolution* (New York: Columbia University Press, 1980), 287–92.

2. Alexis de Tocqueville, *Democracy in America*, ed. J. P. Mayer (Garden City, N.Y.: Doubleday and Company, Inc., 1969), 50, 54.

3. Paul G. Faler, *Mechanics and Manufacturers in the Early Industrial Revolution: Lynn, Massachusetts, 1780–1860* (Albany, N.Y.: State University of New York Press, 1981), chap. 9; Bruce Laurie, *Working People of Philadelphia, 1800–1850* (Philadelphia: Temple University Press, 1980), xi–xii; Anthony F. C. Wallace, *Rockdale: The Growth of an American Village in the Early Industrial Revolution* (New York: Alfred A. Knopf, 1978), 48–51, 59, 63, 255, 386–88.

4. This literature is discussed in James C. Bonner, "Plantation and Farm: The Agricultural South," in Arthur S. Link and Rembert W. Patrick, *Writing Southern History: Essays in Historiography in Honor of Fletcher M. Green* (Baton Rouge: Louisiana State University Press, 1965), 147–60; and in Randolph B. Campbell, "Planters and Plain Folks: The Social Structure of the Antebellum South," in John B. Boles and Evelyn Thomas Nolen, eds., *Interpreting Southern History: Historiographical Essays in Honor of Sanford W. Higginbotham* (Baton Rouge: Louisiana State University Press, 1987), 48–77. On the problem of defining classes, see ibid., 63–66.

5. S. Charles Bolton, "Economic Inequality in the Arkansas Territory," *Journal of Interdisciplinary History* 14 (Winter 1984): 629.

6. The Gini coefficient, which measures inequality based on the entire distribution of wealth and ranges from 0 to 1, was .66 for Jones' data, .73 for Wright's, and .77 for the Arkansas taxpayers. Bolton, "Economic Inequality," 629; Jones, *Wealth of a Nation to Be*, 96–97, 104, 164; Gavin Wright, *The Political Economy of the Cotton South: Households, Markets, and Wealth in the Nineteenth Century* (New York: W. W. Norton & Co., 1978), 26.

7. Dennis H. Wrong, "Social Inequality Without Stratification," Gerald W. Thielbar and Saul D. Feldman, *Issues in Social Stratification* (Boston: Little, Brown & Co., 1972), 91–104; see also Robert E. L. Faris, "The Middle Class from a Sociological Viewpoint," *Issues in Social Stratification*, 26–32.

8. Stanislaw Ossowski, *Class Structure in the Social Consciousness* (New York: Free Press, 1963), 19–60.

9. *Notes of Debates in the Federal Convention of 1787 Reported by James Madison*, intro. Adrienne Koch (New York: W. W. Norton & Co., 1966), 135.

10. Peter Laslett, *The World We Have Lost* (New York: Charles Scribner's Sons, 1965), 29–34; W. Lloyd Warner, "Social Class: Description and Measurement," Thielbar and Feldman, *Issues in Social Inequality*, 17–18.

11. Alexander Hamilton, John Jay, and James Madison, *The Federalist, A Commentary on the Constitution of the United States* (New York: Random House, n.d.), 56.

12. Ossowski, *Class Structure*, 132.

13. Eugene D. Genovese, *The Political Economy of Slavery: Studies in the Economy and Society of the Slave South* (New York: Random House, 1965), 13, 28–29, 32. See also Eugene D. Genovese, *The World the Slaveholders Made: Two Essays in Interpretation* (New York: Random House, 1969); and Eugene D. Genovese, "Race and Class in Southern History: An Appraisal of the Work of Ulrich Bonnell Phillips," *Agricultural History* 41 (1967): 345–56.

14. James Oakes, *The Ruling Race: A History of American Slaveholders* (New York: Norton, 1982), chap 2.

15. Because each taxable slave represented 1.47 slaves of all ages and 1.81 slaves on the census, I have defined small slaveholders as owners of one to four taxable slaves, large slaveholders as those with five to eleven taxable slaves, and planters as those with twelve or more taxable slaves. See Table 1.

16. Harold Woodman, "Economic Reconstruction and the New South," Boles and Nolen, eds., *Interpreting Southern History*, 270.

17. Class structure for taxpayers in 1845 was calculated on the basis of mean property values for 1840. Assessed values for 1845 were significantly lower.

18. Donald Schaefer, "Yeomen Farmers and Economic Democracy: A Study of Wealth and Economic Mobility in the Western Tobacco Region, 1850 to 1860," *Explorations in Economic History* 15 (1978): 421–37. The data is adapted from Table 4 on 428.

19. For a negative test and a discussion of the issues, see Randolph B. Campbell, "Intermittent Slave Ownership: Texas as a Test Case," *Journal of Southern History* 51 (1985): 15–23; James Oakes, "A Response," and Randolph B. Campbell, "A Rejoinder," ibid., 23–30.

20. John Solomon Otto and Ben Wayne Banks, "The Banks Family of Yell County, Arkansas: A 'Plain Folk' Family of the Highlands South," *Arkansas Historical Quarterly* 46 (Summer 1982): 159–60; see also John Solomon Otto, "Slaveholding General Farmers in a 'Cotton County,'" *Agricultural History* 55 (Apr. 1981): 167–78; and John Solomon Otto, "Slavery in the Mountains: Yell County, Arkansas, 1840–1860," 39 (Spring 1980): 35–52.

21. I used the list of delegates in Lonnie J. White, *Politics on the Southwest Frontier: Arkansas Territory, 1819–1836* (Memphis: Memphis State University Press, 1964), 184.

22. *Arkansas Gazette*, Nov. 10, 1935.

23. Ibid., Nov. 11, 1835.

24. Ibid., Jan. 26, 1836. The best discussion of the apportionment issue is in White, *Politics*, 178–81, 185–89. White, however, divides the counties on the basis of his own geographical analysis, ignoring the division indicated by the constitution.

25. The 1840 figure is estimated from the sample of 987 taxpayers, the 1850 and 1860 figures are taken from the census for those years.

26. Woods, *Rebellion and Realignment*, 124.

CHAPTER SEVEN

1. Marvin Myers, *The Jacksonian Persuasion: Politics and Belief* (Stanford: Stanford University Press, 1960), 122–23.

2. Heiskell Small Manuscript Collection, box 2, file 64, University of Arkansas at Little Rock Archives and Special Collections.

3. Carter, *Territorial Papers*, vol. 21, 1207–08.

4. White, *Politics*, 17, 21–22; Ross, *Arkansas Gazette*, 15.

5. White, *Politics*, 21–22, 33–36; Ross, *Arkansas Gazette*, 23–24, 27–29; Robert L. and Pauline H. Jones, "Stephen F. Austin in Arkansas," *Arkansas Historical Quarterly* 25 (1966):336–44.

6. White, *Politics*, 37–46, 52–54; Ross, *Arkansas Gazette*, 48–53, 62–63.

7. White, *Politics*, 66–80; Ross, *Arkansas Gazette*, 66–82.

8. *Arkansas Gazette,* Nov. 6, 1827.

9. White, *Politics,* 83–86, 89–92, 141–57; Josiah H. Shinn, *Pioneers and Makers of Arkansas* (Little Rock, 1908; reprint ed., Baltimore: Genealogical Publishing Company, 1967), 206–08.

10. White, *Politics,* 92–95, 115–25; Ross, *Arkansas Gazette,* 89, 96–97.

11. The Pearson Correlation of Sevier's county vote percentages in the first race with those in the second was .53. The Sevier percentage by county correlated with the percentage of slaves in the county was .43 in 1829 but dropped to -.06 in 1831. The votes are from the *Arkansas Gazette,* Aug. 26, 1829, and Sept. 21, 1831.

12. William F. Pope, *Early Days in Arkansas,* 114.

13. Bertram Wyatt–Brown, *Southern Honor: Ethics and Behavior in the Old South* (New York: Oxford University Press, 1983), 33–34, 350–61.

14. White, *Politics,* 28, 48; William F. Pope, *Early Days in Arkansas* (Little Rock, 1895; reprint ed., Easley, S.C., 1978), 33–37; Andrew Scott to Elizabeth Scott, May 17, 1824, Heiskell Small Manuscript Collection, file 114.

15. Ross, *Arkansas Gazette,* 80–81; Pope, *Early Days,* 37–39; Shin, *Pioneers,* 191–92.

16. White, *Politics,* 112–13; Ross, *Arkansas Gazette,* 95–96; Lonnie J. White, ed., "The Pope Noland Duel of 1831: An Original Letter of C. F. M. Noland to His Father," *Arkansas Historical Quarterly* 22 (1963): 117–23.

17. White, *Politics,* 142–46, 157–58; Pope, *Early Days,* 163–66.

18. Pope, *Early Days,* 40. Ross believes that Crittenden suffered politically from killing Conway, see *Arkansas Gazette,* 86.

19. Cal Ledbetter, Jr., "General James Miller, Hawthorne's Hero in Arkansas," *Arkansas Historical Quarterly* 47 (1988): 101–04.

20. Quoted in White, *Politics,* 62.

21. Ledbetter, "Miller," 105–08; Ross, *Arkansas Gazette,* 61.

22. White, *Politics,* 50–52, 60–65; Ross, *Arkansas Gazette,* 63–70, 73–74.

23. White, *Politics,* 89–91, 98; Ross, *Arkansas Gazette,* 88.

24. White, *Politics,* 127–31; Ross, *Arkansas Gazette,* 97–98.

25. F. Hampton Roy, et al., *How We Lived: Little Rock as an American City* (Little Rock: August House, 1984), 46–48; White, *Politics,* 141–57; Ross, *Arkansas Gazette,* 106.

26. White, *Politics,* 159–72; Ross, *Arkansas Gazette,* 108–18.

27. Carter, *Territorial Papers,* vol. 21, 977–91, esp. 983, 990.

28. *Historical Report of the Secretary of State, Arkansas, 1978* (Winston Bryant, Secretary of State, Arkansas, 1978), vol. 2.

29. Carter, *Territorial Papers,* vol. 19, 148.

30. Ibid., vol. 20, 132, 164–65.

31. Ibid., 775–77.

32. Ibid., vol. 21, 99; ibid., 114–15.

33. Ibid., vol. 21, 402–04, 408–09, 411, 418, 843.

34. Ibid., vol. 19, 232, 555–56; ibid., vol. 21, 93–94, 417–33.

35. Ibid., 822.

36. Ibid., vol. 19, 148, 224, 233, 373–74, 554–55; ibid., vol. 21, 91–93, 108, 419–22, 426.

37. Ibid., vol. 19, 559n.; ibid., vol. 21, 401. See also Moore, "Territorial Arkansas," 171–74; and Julie Ward Longnecker, "A Road Divided: From Memphis to Little Rock Through the Great Mississippi Swamp," *Arkansas Historical Quarterly* 46 (1985): 203–21.

38. Carter, *Territorial Papers*, vol. 21, 116, 400–01, 405–08, 412–17, 807–09, 813–4, 818–19, 831–33, 838–41.

39. Ibid., 406, 424–25, 451–53, 816–18, 828, 833–34, 1105, 1114–15, 1124–25.

40. Ibid., 1122–25.

41. Ibid., vol. 20, 800–01.

42. Moore, "Territorial Arkansas," 368–69.

43. Ross, *Arkansas Gazette*, 90–92.

44. *Arkansas Advocate*, Aug. 18, Nov. 11, 1830. See also ibid., Aug. 25, Sept. 22, Oct. 6, 1830.

45. Ibid., Sept. 8, 1830. See also ibid., Sept. 29, 1830.

46. Ibid., Oct. 13, 31, 1831.

47. *Arkansas Gazette*, Aug. 25, Sept. 15, 1830; see also ibid., July 22, Aug. 18, 1830.

48. Ibid., Oct. 13, 1830

49. Ibid., Apr. 20, 1831.

50. Ibid., "Henry," Aug. 25, 1830; *Arkansas Advocate*, Sept. 8, 1830.

51. *Arkansas Advocate*, May 11, 1831; ibid., Apr. 17, 1833.

52. *Arkansas Gazette*, Jan. 24, 1834.

53. Ibid.

54. Ibid., Jan. 28, 1834. See also "Old Times," ibid., Feb. 4, 1834.

55. White, *Politics*, pp. 166–67, 173–81, 186–89, 192–200.

56. Quoted in Moore, "Territorial Arkansas," 343.

EPILOGUE

1. *Statistics of the U.S. . . . in 1860* (Washington, D.C.: Government Printing Office, 1866), 294. See also Elsie M. Lewis, "Economic Conditions in Ante–bellum Arkansas: 1850–1861," *Arkansas Historical Quarterly* 6 (Autumn 1947): 256–74.

2. Richard A. Easterlin, "Regional Income Trends, 1840–1950," in Seymour E. Harris, ed., *American Economic History* (New York, McGraw–Hill Book Company, Inc., 1961), 528; Harold D. Woodman, "Economic Reconstruction and the Rise of the New South, 1865–1900," Boles and Nolen, eds., *Interpreting Southern History*, 262–64.

3. *Historical Statistics of the United States, Colonial Times to the Present* (Washington, D.C., 1975), vol. 1, 243; U.S. Bureau of the Census, *Statistical Abstract of the United States: 1990* (110th edition, Washington, D.C., 1990), 437.

4. Lee A. Dew, "'On a Slow Train Through Arkansaw'—The Negative Image of Arkansas in the Early Twentieth Century," *Arkansas Historical Quarterly* 39 (Summer 1980): 125–35; Foy Lisenby, "A Survey of Arkansas' Image Problem," *Arkansas Historical Quarterly* 30 (Spring 1971): 61–71.

Index

Philbrook, Nathaniel, 65
Phillips County:
    agricultural production, 39, 45; creation
        of, 23; naming of, 60
Phillips, Sylvanus, 60-61
Phillips, Ulrich B., 91
Pitman, Philip, 14, 16
Plain Folk of the Old South, 47
planter class, 3–4, 49, 91, 95–96, 99–100;
    political influence, 101–102, 124
Poke Bayou, 22, 31–32, 113
poll tax, 41, 92
Pope County, 55
Pope, John, 111–13
Pope, William F., 108–109
population, 42, 51; Arkansas Post, 14, 16–
    17; growth, 20–24, 28–29, 41; in repre-
    sentation, 100–101; Native Americans,
    8–9, 11, 14–15, 18; slave, 29, 42, 45, 53,
    98; statehood, 114, 117–20; women, 82;
potatoes, 32, 45, 47, 53
Potter, David, 3–4, 102, 123
Potts Tavern, 55
Potts, Kirkbride, 55
Pottsville, 55
Pratz, Le Page du, 14
preemption, 58, 72–73, 115;
Preemption act of April 12, 1814, 58;
    Bowie claims, 70; Little Rock, 64–66
Preston, Isaac T., 68–70
public land system, 57–58; 73–75; 114–5
Pulaski County, 23, 27, 39,

Quapaw:
    at Arkansas Post, 14–15, 18; and the
        French, 11–12; removal, 25, 114, 122
Quiguate, 10

Ranjel, Rodrigo, 10
Rector, Elias, 35, 104
Rector, Wharton, 104–105
Rector, William, 58, 106
Red River Raft, 29, 39, 74, 116
Red River, 11, 39, 45
Reed, Opie, 124
Roane, Sam, 68–72
Roberts, Mary, 83
Roberts, Mason, 83

Robertson, George, 24
Rohrbough, Malcolm J., 3
Rorer, David, 67
Ruling Race, The, 95
Russell, William, 22, 60–61, 64–66

Saline County, 49–50, 101
Salle, Rene-Robert Cavelier de Sieur la,
    7, 12
Sampeyreac, Bernardo, 70
Schoolcraft, Henry, 30–32, 78
Scott County, 47 113
Scott, Andrew, 108, 113
Searcy County, 113
Searcy, Richard, 67, 107
Selden, John, 108
Seminole Wars, 105
Senex, 100, 102
Sevier County, 45, 113
Sevier, Ambrose Hundley:
    Bowie claims, 70, 72; Cherokee dona-
        tion claims, 67; dueling, 108–09;
        Family, the, 104–05; political career,
        107–08, 111–13; on statehood, 118–20
Sevier, John, 107, 112
sheep, 18, 53, 62, 84
Shreve, Henry, 29, 74
slaveholders, 91, 95–99, 102, 120; Arkansas
    County, 52–53; Arkansas Post, 14, 16
slavery:
    Arkansas County, 51–53; and cattle
        ownership, 48–49; sectionalism, 42–
        45, 75, 100–102, 107, 120; statehood,
        24, 118–9;
slaves:
    Arkansas Post, 14, 16–18, 20; as wealth,
        54–55, 90; Native American, 10, 15;
        population growth, 50–51; ratio of
        women, 29
Smith, Daniel Scott, 81
social class, 90–91, 93–98, 102
Southwest Trail, 21, 22, 23, 31, 33. See also
    Military Road
Spanish:
    administration, 15–16; exploration 9–11;
        land claims 59–62, 68, 70–72
Spring River, 22
St, Francis River, 14, 59, 116
St. Louis, 16, 23

Bowie claims, 71–72; Cherokee donation claims, 67–68; Conway, Henry
support, 106–7; Pope, John, 111–2; on
agriculture, 40–41; on Choctaw
Treaty, 27–28; on military bounties,
63; on statehood, 116–9
Woodward, Jane, 87
Wright, Carroll, 42
Wright, Gavin, 92